The Christ Impulse and the Development of the Ego-Consciousness

A Course of Seven Lectures
BY DR. RUDOLF STEINER

(Shorthand Report unrevised by the Lecturer)

LONDON :
ANTHROPOSOPHICAL PUBLISHING Co.
46, GLOUCESTER PLACE, W.1

Authorised Translation
Edited by H. Collison

Printed in Guernsey by the Star and Gazette Co., Ltd.

CONTENTS

SYNOPSIS OF CONTENTS.

The following synopsis of contents is intended for the convenience of students, and is in no sense authoritative.

descent. Reason for lies, disease, death. The Golden Age or Krita juga. The Silver age or Treta juga. The Bronze age or Dvapara juga. The Dark Age or Kali juga, beginning 3101 B.C. From Lemuria to Mount Sinai was the power to choose good or evil. Sin. The ten commandments tell man how an Ego should behave. The Poor in Spirit. The Christ Impulse. The Etheric body. Illness. The Inner Comforter. The Astral body. Indifference to things of the Earth. Sentient Soul. Blessed are the Just. The Intellectual Soul. Blessed are those who can feel with others, for others shall feel with them. By the Sermon on the Mount Christ turns within man what the Commandments had dictated from outside. Tacitus. Necessity for Christ to descend during the darkest time. The Kali juga or Dark age ended with the 19th century. Christ will not return in the flesh. A new era and a new understanding are being prepared for 1930 onwards. Materialism will spread to spiritual conceptions.

LECTURE 4. Reason for Christ's descent to physical plane. Zarathustra. The Generations. Itiel, Lemuel. Ben Jage. Agur. Jedidjah. Kohelet. Salomo. Old dreamy clairvoyance. Unconscious of ego outside. Ecstasy in company with good spirits changes to obsession by bad spirits. ' Blessed ' means ' God-filled '. The Beatitudes. Further individual developments after 1930. The near future and its possibilities and dangers. The Event of Damascus. The danger of preaching a physical return. Christ is here always even unto the end of the world. False Messiahs.

LECTURE 5. Difference between North, South and Christian Initiation. Duality and unity. Male and female Duality in Universe. Duality in man. Sun and Earth. Head and Limbs. Original uniform being divided into man and woman. Woman crystallises an earlier spiritual form. Man is a caricature of what should be a future form. Both male and female forms are distortions. The female brain is more pliable and spiritual. A woman corresponds to a comet which enters our existence with laws pertaining to Old Moon. It carries a former condition into a later. The Moon-like man, is a present caricature of the Jupiter condition. The above applies to the male in the woman and to the female in the man. Man is male in physical but female in etheric. Woman the reverse. Spiritual science in Paris, 1906, declared comets must possess cyonagen. This has now been discovered true by spectro-analysis. The comet appears in the regular life of cosmos, like the new-born child arriving in the well ordered home of humdrum matrimony. Like children, some comets are good, some bad. Halley's comet gives an impulse to materialism. ' Signs from the Heavens.' In the next 2,500 years the etheric realm will be added to our perception, so that our environment will look quite different. The fairy land of Shamballa.

The Christ Impulse and the Development of the Ego-Consciousness

BY DR. RUDOLF STEINER

LECTURE 1.

Berlin, 25th October, 1909.

THE SPHERE OF THE BODHISATTVAS

To-DAY, on the occasion of our General Meeting, I feel it incumbent upon me to speak upon a very sublime subject with which man is concerned. You must allow me to begin by mentioning once again that it is necessary for us to grow accustomed to speak in such a way on these subjects, that we must not rest satisfied with a one-sided rendering of the particulars connected with the higher world, as regards the general idea of the Bodhisattvas and their mission. We must accustom ourselves here to penetrate from the abstract into the concrete and to try, with the help of the ideas and sentiments which we have acquired from our sincere and loving study of life, to press through even to the sublime subjects pertaining to the Bodhisattvas. In doing this we must not merely accept the facts communicated to us, but try to a certain extent to understand them. For this reason I intend in this lecture to-day to begin by giving some description of the idea men had of the Bodhisattvas and of how that idea moved through the world.

We cannot really understand what a Bodhisattva is, without going somewhat deeply into the progressive course of man's evolution, and calling to mind some of the things we have heard in the last few years. Let us consider the nature of this progress. After the great Atlantean catastrophe humanity went through the period of the Old Indian civilisation, during which the great Rishis were the teachers of man. Then followed the period of the Old Persian civilisation ; then that of the Egypto-Chaldean civilisation, then the Graeco-Latin period—up to our own, which is the fifth period of civilisation of the Post-Atlantean age. The purpose of these periods is the progressive development of humanity from one form of life to another. Progress is not made only in what is generally described in external history ; for if we take great periods of time, we find that all the sentiments and feelings, all the conceptions and ideas of men, alter and are renewed in the course of the development of humanity. What would be the use of advocating the idea of re-embodiment or reincarnation, if we did not know this ? What use would it be for our soul to come back over and over again into an earthly body, unless it were to learn something new each time—and not only to have new experiences, but to learn to feel differently ? Even the capacities of man, the intimacies of his soul-life, are each time renewed and altered. This makes it possible for the soul to do more than merely ascend stage by stage as though up a series of steps, for each time it meets with new opportunities, through the altered conditions of life, of acquiring something new on earth. The soul is not merely guided from one incarnation to another by its sins and errors ; but as our earth alters in every one of its conditions of life, so our souls can each time add something new from without. Therefore the soul progresses from incarnation to incarnation, but also from one period of civilisation to another. It would not, however, be able to progress and develop, were it not that those Beings who had already reached a high development, and were in some way or other above the ordinary humanity, had taken care that something new might always flow into earthly civilisation. In other words, we could not have advanced if there had not been great Teachers at work who, on account of their higher development, were able to receive the experiences from the higher worlds and carry them down to the scene of action of the life of earthly culture. There have always been such Beings in the development of our earth. (I am only speaking to-day of the Post-Atlantean development) and these Beings were in certain respects the Teachers of the rest. We can only understand the nature of these Teachers of humanity if we are clear as to the way humanity itself progresses.

You will have heard the two Lectures just given by Dr. Unger, on the Ego in its relation to the Non-Ego in its comprehension of itself considered according to the theory of Knowledge. Now do you suppose that what you then heard rendered by human lips and human thinking, could have been heard in this form 2,500 years ago ? It would have been impossible in any part of the earth to speak about the Ego in this form of pure thought. Suppose some individuality 2,500 years ago had desired to incarnate into our earth-life, having made up its mind beforehand to speak of the Ego in that special way, well, it could not have done so ! Anyone who supposes that anything of the kind could have been uttered by human lips, 2,500 years ago, entirely fails to recognise the actual progress and alteration in the development of civilisation since that time. For this to be possible it would not only be necessary for an individuality to resolve to incarnate in a human body, but it would also have been necessary that our earth in her evolution should have produced a human body with a particular sort of brain, so that the truths, which in the higher worlds are quite of a different nature, could in that particular brain take the form which we call ' pure thought.' For the way in which Dr. Unger spoke of the Ego we call the form of pure thought. 2,500 years ago there would have been no human brain capable of being an instrument for translating these truths into such thoughts. The Beings who wish to descend to our earth must make use of the bodies which this earth-cycle itself produces. Our earth, however, throughout the different periods of civilisation has always brought forth bodies with ever different organisations ; only in our fifth Post-Atlantean epoch of civilisation, has it become possible to speak in the form of pure thought—the human race having pro-

2

duced the necessary bodies. Even in the Graeco-Latin age it would not yet have been possible to speak like that along the lines of the theory of knowledge, for there would have been no instrument there to translate such thoughts into human language. That precisely is the task of our fifth Post-Atlantean period ; it must gradually form the physical organisation of man into an instrument through which those truths, which in other ages were grasped in quite other forms, can flow in ever purer and purer thought. We will take another example. When a man considers the question of good and evil at the present day, hesitating as to whether he should or should not do a certain thing, he says that a kind of inner voice speaks, telling him : ' You ought not to do this. You ought to do that ! ' and that this has nothing to do with any outer law. If we listen to this inner voice, we distinguish in it a certain impulse, an incitement to act in a certain way in a given case. We call this inner voice conscience. If a man is of the opinion that the different periods of man's development were all exactly alike, he might easily believe that as long as man has inhabited the earth, conscience has always existed. That would not be correct. We can, so to speak, prove historically that there was a beginning to the time when men began to speak of conscience. When this was, is clearly evident. It lay between the periods of two tragic poets : Æschylos, who was born in the sixth century before our era, and Euripides, who was born in the fifth century. You will find no mention of conscience previous to this. Even in Æschylos you will not as yet find what could be called the inner voice ; what he writes of, still took the form of an astral, pictorial apparition ; the Furies or Erinyes, vengeful beings, appeared to men. The time came, however, when the astral perception of the Furies was replaced by the inner voice of conscience. Even in the Graeco-Latin period, in which a dim astral perception was still present, a man who had committed a wrong could perceive that every wrong act created astral forms in his environment, whose presence filled him with anxiety and fear as to what he had done. Those forms were man's educators at that time ; they gave him his impulses. When he lost the last remains of his astral clairvoyance, this perception was replaced by the invisible voice of conscience ; that means, that what was at first outside, then entered into the soul and became one of the forces now within it. The alteration that has taken place in mankind in the course of development comes from the fact that the external instrument of man, in which he seeks embodiment, has changed. Five thousand years ago, when a human soul did something wrong, the Furies were perceived ; it could not then have heard the Voice of Conscience. In this way it learnt to establish an inner relation to good and evil. This same soul was born again and again, and at last it was born into a body possessing an organisation in which the quality of conscience could approach it. In a future cycle of human development other forms and other capacities will be experienced in the soul.

I have repeatedly laid stress on the fact that no one who really understands Anthroposophy will take up the dogmatic attitude of asserting that the form in which this is given out to-day will be permanent and will suffice for the humanity of all future time. Such is not the case. In 2,500 years' time the same truths will not be revealed in this form, but in a different form, according to the instruments then existing. If you bear this in mind, it will be clear to you that humanity must be spoken to in a different manner in each successive age and that the attitude of the great Teachers towards the capacities and qualities of man must likewise differ. This signifies that the great Teachers themselves undergo development from one cycle to another, from one age to another. In the ages through which humanity progresses, we find going on above man, as it were, a progressive evolution of the great Teachers of humanity. Just as man passes through certain stages and then reaches a certain turning-point, so likewise do the Great Teachers.

We are now living in the fifth period of our Post-Atlantean epoch of civilisation. This is in a certain sense, a recapitulation of the third, of the Egypto-Chaldean period. The sixth will, in like manner, recapitulate the Old Persian, and the seventh will recapitulate the Old Indian. Thus do the various cycles overlap each other. The fourth period will not be recapitulated; it stands in the middle—sufficient unto itself, as we might say. What does this mean? It means that what men experienced in the Graeco-Latin period they only need go through once in an epoch of civilisation; not that they were only once incarnated in it, but that they only experience that period in one form. What was experienced in the Egypto-Chaldean period is being recapitulated now; it will thus be experienced in a two-fold form. There are certain stages of development which betoken a sort of crisis; while other periods are in certain respects like one another, the one recapitulating the other, not in the same way, but in a different form. The manner of man's development in the Post-Atlantean age is this: he went through a certain number of incarnations in the Old Indian period—and will go through a certain number in the seventh period, and these latter will resemble the former. A like resemblance will exist between the second and the sixth—and between the third and the fifth periods. Between these—in the fourth period—there are a number of incarnations, which resemble no other, and which therefore do not signify a transition. Man goes through a descending and an ascending development. The great Teachers of humanity also go through a period of descent and one of ascent, and differ absolutely at the different periods.

Now as man in the first Post-Atlantean period had quite different capacities from those he acquired later, he had to be instructed in quite a different way. To what do we owe the fact that in our time wisdom can be clothed in the concise forms of pure thought? We owe this to the circumstance that in our period of development the chief and average quality that is being developed is the consciousness [1] soul. In the Graeco-Latin period the intellectual soul or mind was being developed, in the Egyptio-Chaldean the sentient soul, in the Old Persian the sentient body, and in the Old Indian the etheric body;—as the chief factor in their culture, of course. What the consciousness-soul is to us, that the etheric body was to the inhabitants of Old India. They had therefore quite a different mode of grasping and understanding. If you had spoken to the Old Indian in forms of pure thought, he would not have had the faintest idea what you meant. To him such words would have been mere sounds, without meaning. The great Teachers could not have taught the Old Indians

[1] Since 1923 called by Dr. Steiner " The Spiritual Soul."

4

by communicating wisdom to them in the form of pure thought, nor could they have explained it by word of mouth. To the Old Indians the Great Teachers said very little; for at the stage which the etheric body had then reached people were not receptive to the word which enclosed the thought. It is very difficult for people of our day to imagine how teaching could have taken place under those conditions. Very little indeed was spoken; rather did the listening soul recognise in the nuances of the sound, in the way a word was uttered, what flowed down from the spiritual world. That, however, was not the chief thing. The word was, so to speak, only the call to attention, the signal, that a relationship must now be established between the teacher and the hearer. In the earliest times of the Old Indian period the word was hardly more than when we ring a bell as a sign that something is about to begin. It was a crystallising point around which were woven the indescribable, spiritual currents which passed from the teacher to his pupil. What was of greatest importance was what the teacher saw, in his inner personality. It did not matter what he said; the qualities of his soul were of the greatest importance; for a sort of inspiration passed over from him to the pupil. The latter, having in particular developed the etheric body, the teacher had to address himself specially to that; and it was much easier to understand what the teacher himself was, than anything spoken. Before they could understand the spoken word, men had to pass through the subsequent periods of civilisation. It was therefore not necessary for any one of the great Teachers of the Old Indians to have a particularly developed intellectual or consciousness soul, for such would have been at that time an instrument of which he could make no use. One thing, however, was necessary in these great Teachers: their own etheric bodies had to be at a more advanced stage of development than were those of the people. If a great teacher had stood at the same stage of development as they, he could not have had much effect upon them; he could not have communicated messages from a higher world, nor given an impulse for progress. In a certain sense what man was to grow to in the future, had first to be brought to him. The Indian teacher had to anticipate, as it were, what the others would only be able to acquire in the subsequent period of civilisation, that of the Old Persians. What the ordinary man in the Old Persian period would take in through the sentient body, that the Great Teacher of the Indians had to communicate through the etheric body. That means that the etheric body of such a teacher must not work like those of other men, it had to work as the sentient body was to do in the Persian civilisation. If a seer, in the present sense of the word, had come in contact with one of the great Indian teachers, he would have said: "What sort of etheric body is that?" For such an etheric body would have looked like an astral body of the Old Persian period.

It was, however, no such simple matter for such an etheric body to have worked as an astral body of a later period. It could not have been brought about at that time by any advanced stage of development. It could only be made possible by the descent of a Being who had already reached a further stage than the others, and who incarnated in a human body which was really neither suited to nor well adapted to him, but which he was obliged to enter to make himself understood by the others. Outwardly he looked like other men, but

5

inwardly he was quite different. To judge of such an individual by his outer aspect would mean to deceive oneself utterly ; for while the outer appearance of ordinary persons harmonises with their inner being, in the case of these Teachers it was in complete contradiction. Here we have an individuality, who, as far as he himself was concerned, had no longer any need to come down to earth at all, but who descended to a certain stage and took his place among the Old Indian people, to teach them. He descended willingly, and incarnated in human form, though he was a different Being altogether. He was an individual of such a nature that the destiny to which a normal man—as man—is subject, did not affect him. A Teacher of this kind would live in a body having an external destiny, yet he would have no part in that destiny ; he lived in that body as in a house. When that body died, death for him was a very different experience from what it is for other men. Birth, too, and the experiences between birth and death were quite different for him. Hence also such a Being worked in quite a different way in this human instrument. Let us picture to ourselves in what way such an individuality used the brain, for instance. For even if he was able to perceive through the astral body, yet the brain which indeed was otherwise organised, still had to be used as an instrument to observe the pictures through which perceptions were received. There were, therefore, two human types ; the one, who used his brain as an ordinary human being, and the Teacher type, who did not use his brain at all in the ordinary way, but in a certain sense left it unused. A great Teacher did not need to use the brain in all its details; he knew things that other people could only learn through the instrument of the brain. It was not a real, earthly incarnation as such ; it was not a real incarnation of a human being in the ordinary sense. It represented a sort of double nature ; a spiritual being lived in this organisation. There were such Beings also in the later Persian and in the Egyptian periods. It was always the case that in their individuality they towered far above the stature of their human organisation. They were not wholly contained within it. For that reason they were able to work upon the rest of the people in those olden times. This state of things continued down to the time when, in the Graeco-Latin period, an important crisis occurred in the development of mankind.

Now in the Graeco-Latin age the intellectual soul or mind[1] began gradually to form inner faculties. Whereas in the time preceding this the chief things flowed in from outside, so to speak—as we saw in the example of the Furies, when men had avenging beings around them but not within them—in the Graeco-Latin period something began to flow from within, towards the great Teachers. In this way quite new conditions were established. Formerly, Beings from the Higher Worlds descended and found a state of things which enabled them to say : " It is not necessary for us completely to enter the human organisation ; for we can do our work by carrying down to men what they cannot otherwise obtain, and causing that to flow into them from the Higher Worlds." At that time it was not yet necessary for man to contribute anything, there was no need for him to bring anything to meet the great Teachers. But if the great Teachers had gone on with this policy, it might have occurred—from the fourth Period onwards—that one of these great Individualities would have

[1] Mind in the sense of ' I have a mind to do a thing.'

descended into some part of the earth and found there something which did not exist above. As long as the Furies, the avenging spirits, were visible, men could turn their attention away from what was to be found on earth. Now, however, came something quite new—conscience. That was unknown to the spirits above; there was no possibility up there of observing it. It came as something quite new to them. In other words, in the fourth period of Post-Atlantean civilisation the necessity arose for these great Teachers actually to descend to the stage of man, therein to learn what it was that was coming up to meet them out of the human souls. Now began the time when it would not do for them not to share to some extent in the qualities inherent in man. Let us now observe that significant Being, whom in his earthly incarnation we know as Gautama Buddha.

Gautama Buddha was a Being who had always been able to incarnate in the earthly bodies of the various periods of civilisation, without having had to use everything in this human organisation. It had not been necessary for this Being to go through real human incarnations. Now, however, came an important turning-point for the Bodhisattva; it now became necessary for him to make himself acquainted with all the destinies of the human organisation within an earthly body which he was to enter. He was to experience something which could only be experienced in an earthly body; and because he was such a high Individuality, this one incarnation was sufficient for him to see all that a human body can develop. Other people have to evolve the inner capacities gradually, throughout the fourth, fifth, sixth, and seventh periods; but Buddha could experience in this one incarnation all that it was possible to evolve. In his incarnation as Gautama Buddha he saw, in advance, the first germ of what was to arise in man as conscience, which will become greater and greater as time goes on. He was therefore able to re-ascend into the spiritual world directly after that incarnation; there was no need for him to go through another. What man will, in a certain sphere evolve out of himself during future cycles, Buddha was able to give in this one incarnation, as a great directing force. This came about through the event which has been described as the "sitting under the Bodhi-tree." He then gave forth—in accordance with his special mission—the teaching of compassion and love contained in the eight-fold path. This great Ethic of humanity which men will acquire as their own during the civilisations yet to come, was laid down as a basic force in the mind of the Buddha who descended at that time, and from Bodhisattva became Buddha, which means that he really rose a stage higher, for he learnt through his descent.

That, in different words, describes that great event in Eastern civilisation known as " the Bodhisattva becoming Buddha." When this Bodhisattva, who had never really incarnated, was 29 years of age, his individuality fully entered the son of Suddhodana; not having fully had possession of him. He then experienced the great human teaching of compassion and love. Why did this Bodhisattva, who then became Buddha, incarnate in this people? Why not in the Graeco-Latin people?

If this Bodhisattva was really to become the Buddha of the fourth Post-Atlantean period of civilisation, he had to bring in something new for the future. When the consciousness-or spiritual-soul has been fully developed, man will, by its means, gradually become sufficiently ripe to recognise of himself the great impetus given by Buddha. At a time when man had only developed the intellectual soul, it was necessary that Buddha should already have developed the spiritual soul. He had so to use the physical instrument of the brain that he was complete master of it ; and this in quite a different fashion than could have been done by one who might have progressed in advance as far as the Graeco-Latin period of civilisation. The Graeco-Latin brain would have been too hard for him to use. It would only have enabled him to develop the intellectual or mind [1] soul, whereas he had to develop the spiritual soul. For that he required a brain that had remained softer. He made use of the soul that was only to develop later, in an instrument that had been used by man in earlier times and had been retained by the Indian people. Here again we have a recapitulation : Buddha repeated a human organisation belonging to earlier times, together with a soul-capacity belonging to times yet to come. The events that take place in the evolution of humanity are to this extent, of the nature of a necessity. In the 5th to the 6th century before our era, Buddha had the task of introducing the spiritual-soul into the organisation of man. He, as a single individual, could not, however, take over the whole task of doing all that was necessary in order that the spiritual-soul might prepare itself in the right way from the 5th century onward. His own particular mission only comprised one part of that task : that of bringing to man the doctrine of Compassion and Love. Other teachers of humanity would have other tasks. This part of the Ethics of Humanity, the ethic of Love and Compassion, was first introduced by Buddha, and its vibrations still endure ; but humanity must in future develop a number of other qualities besides these, as, for instance, that of thinking in forms of pure thought, in crystal-clear thoughts. It was no part of Buddha's mission to build up thoughts, to add one clear thought to another. His task was to form and establish that which leads man of his own accord to find the eight-fold path.

So there had to be another Teacher of humanity having quite different faculties, one who carried down a different stream of spiritual life from the higher spiritual worlds into this world. To this other individuality was given the task of carrying down what is gradually showing itself, in mankind to-day, as the faculty of logical thought. A Teacher had to be found, able to carry down what makes it possible for man to express himself in forms of pure thought; for logical thought itself only developed as time went on. What Buddha accomplished had to be carried into the intellectual- or mind-soul. This soul, through its position between the sentient soul and the consciousness- or spiritual-soul, possesses the peculiar attribute of not having to recapitulate anything. The Old Indian epoch will be repeated in the seventh, the Old Persian in the sixth, the Egyptian in our own ; but just as the fourth epoch stands alone, apart from the others, so does the intellectual- or mind-soul. The forces necessary for our intellectual faculties which only appear in the spiritual-soul, could not be developed in the intellectual soul ; although these were only to appear later, they had to be laid down in germ and stimulated at an earlier period.

[1] Mind in the sense of ' I have a mind to do a thing.'

In other words : the impulse for logical thinking had to be given before the Buddha gave the impulse for Conscience. Conscience was to be organised into man in the fourth epoch ; conscious, pure thinking was to develop in the consciousness- or spiritual-soul in the fifth epoch, but had to be laid down in the third epoch of civilisation, as the germ for what we are evolving now. That is why that other Great Teacher had the task of instilling into the sentient soul the forces which now appear as pure thought. It is therefore easy to see that the difference between this Teacher and the normal man, was even greater than it was in Buddha. Something had to be aroused in the sentient soul which did not as yet exist in any living man. Ideas or conceptions would not have helped to develop this ; therefore although this Individuality had the task of laying the germ of certain faculties, he could not himself make any use of them. That would have been impossible. He had to employ other, quite different, forces.

I explained this morning (in the second lecture on " Anthroposophy ") that certain forces working through the power of vision on the sentient soul, will at a higher stage become conscious forces, and will then appear in the form of thought. If that great Teacher-Individuality was able so to stimulate the sentient-soul that the forces of thought could penetrate it, in somewhat the same way as life subconsciously penetrated it through the act of vision— without the least realising it, that Teacher could then achieve something. This could only be done in one way. To stimulate the sentient soul and instil into it, so to speak, the power of thought, this Individuality had to work in a very special way. He had to give his instruction, not in conceptions—but through music ! Music engenders forces which set free in the sentient soul something, which, when it rises into the consciousness and has been worked upon by the spiritual soul, becomes logical thinking. This music came forth from a mighty Being, who taught through music. You will think this strange, and may perhaps not believe it possible, yet such was the case. Before the Graeco-Latin age, in certain parts of Europe, there existed an ancient culture among those peoples who had remained behind as regards the qualities strongly developed in the East. In those parts of Europe the people were not able to think much, for their development had been of quite a different nature ; they had but little of the forces of the intellectual soul. Their sentient soul, however, was very receptive to what proceeded from the impulses of a special kind of music, which was not the same as our music to-day. We thus go back to a time in Europe when there was what we might call an ancient " musical culture "— a time when not only the " Bards " were the teachers, as they were later, when these things had already fallen into decadence, but when a music full of enchant- ment passed through all those parts of Europe. In the third epoch of civilisa- tion (i.e., the Egyptian) there was a profound musical culture in Europe, and the minds of those peoples who were waiting quietly for what they were destined to carry out later, were receptive in a particular way to the effects of music. These effects worked upon the sentient soul in a similar way to that in which the thought-substance works upon it through the eyes. Thus did music work on the physical plane ; but the sentient soul had the subconscious feeling : " This comes from the same regions as the Light." Music—the song from the realms of Light !

Once upon a time there was a primeval Teacher in the civilised parts of Europe—a primeval Teacher who in this sense was a primeval Bard, the pioneer of all the ancient Bards and minstrels. He taught on the physical plane by means of music, and he taught in such a way that something was thereby communicated to the sentient-soul, which was like the rising and shining of a sun. What tradition has retained concerning this great Teacher was later on gathered together by the Greeks—who were still influenced by him from the West as they were influenced in a different way from the East. This was embodied in their conception of Apollo, who was a Sun-God and at the same time the God of music. This figure of Apollo dates back, however, to that great Teacher of primeval times, who put into the human soul the faculty which appears to-day as the power of clear thinking.

The Greeks also tell of a pupil of this Great Teacher of humanity—of one who became a pupil in a very special way. How could anyone become the " pupil " of this Being ?

In those bygone times, when this Being was to work in the manner just described, he was not, of course, encompassed in the physical organisation ; he transcended that which walks the earth as physical man. A man with an ordinary sentient-soul might have been receptive to the effects of the music, but he could not have aroused them in others. A higher Individuality had come down and was like the radiance of what lived in the cosmos outside. It became necessary, however, that in the fourth Post-Atlantean epoch of civilisation, in the Graeco-Latin period, he should descend again—that he should descend to the human stage and make use of all the faculties that are in man. Yet, although he made use, so to speak, of all the human faculties, he could not quite descend. For, in order to bring about what I have described, he required faculties transcending those possessed by a human organisation in the fourth post-Atlantean period. The effects of this music even then included what was to be found in the spiritual soul ; and it could not at that time have lived in an individuality organised only for the intellectual soul. Hence, although incarnated in such a form, he still had to hold something back. His incarnation in the fourth epoch was such, that although he completely filled the whole human form, yet he as man, dwelling within that form, had, as it were, something within him that extended far beyond it ; he knew something of a spiritual world, but he could not make use of this knowledge. He had a soul which extended beyond his body. Humanly speaking, there was something tragic in the fact that the Individuality who had acted as a great Teacher in the third epoch of civilisation, should have had to incarnate again in a form in which his soul was to a great extent outside it—and yet that he could not make any use of this superior and unusual faculty of soul. This kind of incarnation was called a " Son of Apollo ", because that which had dwelt on earth before, was reincarnated in a very complicated and not in a direct way. A Son of Apollo bore within him as soul what Mysticism designates by the symbol of the ' feminine ' element ; he could not bear all of it within him, because it was in another world. His own feminine soul element was itself in another world to which he had no access but for which he longed, because a part of himself was there. This marvellous inner tragedy of the reincarnated Teacher

10

of former times has been wonderfully preserved in Greek Mythology under the name of ' Orpheus '—the name given to the reincarnated Apollo, or " Son of Apollo."

This tragedy of the soul is represented in a marvellous way in the figures of ' Orpheus and Eurydice '. Eurydice was soon torn from Orpheus. She dwelt in another world ; but Orpheus still had the power, through his music, of teaching the beings of the nether world. He obtained permission from them to take Eurydice back with him. But he must not look around him ; for that would mean inner death ;—at all events it would bring about a loss of what he formerly was and which he cannot now take into himself.

Thus in this incarnation of Apollo as Orpheus, we have again a sort of descent of a Bodhisattva—if we may use this Eastern term—to Buddha-hood. We might quote a number of such Beings who stand out from age to age as the great Teachers of humanity and who always had a very special experience at the time of their deepest descent. The Buddha experiences the bliss of in-spiring the whole of humanity. That Bodhisattva whose memory is preserved externally under the name of ' Apollo,' had an individual experience : he was to prepare the individuality, the quality of the Ego. He experiences the tragedy of the Ego ; he experiences the fact that this ego is, in the present state of man as regards this attribute of his, not entirely with him. Man is strug-gling up to the higher ego. That was foreshadowed for the Greeks by the Buddha or Bodhisattva in Orpheus.

These particulars furnish us with a characterisation of the great Teachers of humanity and we are then able to form a picture in our minds. If you summarise what I have said, you will find that I have all along been speaking of those Beings who formed the sentient-soul and the spiritual-soul in a particular way as inner faculties—faculties which must draw into man from within. As we are now surveying this one period we can only for the moment consider two of these Beings, those who formed the sentient soul. But there are many such, for the inner nature of man evolved gradually, stage by stage.

Let us now compare yet another Being with that which affects the inner nature of man, so to speak. For indeed we cannot but say to ourselves : If there is a constant succession of Teachers who supply the progressing and developing inner faculties of man with spiritual food from the higher regions, there must be other Individualities who accomplish other work and above all take part in the changes in the earth itself and in what evolves from one age to another. When the Buddha influenced the intellectual soul from within, so to speak, through the consciousness or spiritual soul in the fourth period of civilisa-tion, it must also be influenced from without. Something had to approach the intellectual soul from without. This Being had to approach from another side and to work in quite a different way. A Teacher such as those we have been describing, had, when he appeared among men, to pour into their inner being what he had to bring down from higher regions. He was a Teacher. What had the other Being to do, who was to bring the earth forward, so that it developed further from one generation to another ? He was not only to in-fluence the inner being of man to develop this or that faculty within him, but He Himself, as Being, had to descend to the earth. He who was to descend, was not merely to *teach* the intellectual soul, but to form it. One had to appear who was to form that soul and who was Himself to be its direct expression in the fourth period, that eminent period that stands alone in the middle. This Being had to come from quite a different side. He had to draw into human nature itself, to incarnate within it. The Bodhisattvas transformed the inner nature of man ; this Being transformed his whole nature. He made it possible for the Teachers to find a suitable soil on which to work in the future. He transformed the whole human being. We must recollect how the different souls in man build themselves into the different bodies : the sentient soul into the sentient body, the intellectual into the etheric body and the spiritual soul into the physical body. The field of action of the Bodhisattvas is there where the spiritual soul builds itself into the physical body. That is where they lay hold of man from the one side. Where the intellectual- or mind-soul works into the etheric body, another Being, in the fourth period, influenced man from another side. When did he do this ? It was accomplished at the time when the etheric body in man could be directly affected,—when that Being whom we have described more closely as Jesus of Nazareth, forsook the physical body at the moment of the Baptism in Jordan. When that whole body was immersed, whereby occurred what we have described as a ' shock,' the Christ-Being sank down into that etheric body. That is the Individuality Who comes from quite a different side and is of quite a different nature. Whereas in the case of the other great Leaders of humanity we have, in a sense, to do with more highly evolved human beings, men who have at least once been subject to all the fate of a man,—of Christ that cannot be said. What is the lowest principle of the Christ-Being ? Counting from below, it is the etheric body. That means that when some day man, through Spirit-Self, shall have transformed his whole astral body and will set to work on his etheric body, he will then be working in an element in which the Christ once worked in the same way. Christ gives an impulse of the most powerful kind, which will continue to work on into the future, and which man will only reach when he begins to work at the trans-mutation of his etheric body in a conscious way.

In his journey through life, man starts from birth, or even from conception, and travels on till death ; from death to his next birth is another journey. On his way from death to a new birth he first passes through the astral world ; then through what we call the lower part of the Devachanic world, and after that through the higher Devachanic world. Or, using the European terms, we call the physical world the little world or the world of mental powers, of intelligence ; the astral world is called the elemental world ; the lower Devachan the heavenly world, and the Higher world is the world of reason, of discernment, of discretion. The European mind is only gradually evolving to the point where the true expressions may be found in its language. Therefore, what lies beyond the Devachanic world has been given a religious colouring and is called the ' world of Providence '—which is the same as the Buddhi-plane. What is beyond that again could indeed be seen by the old clairvoyant vision, and ancient tradition tells of it ; in the European languages no name could be formed for it.—Only in our present day can the seer once more work his way up to that world which is above and beyond the World of Providence. European languages cannot truly give a name to this world. This world does indeed exist ; but thought is not yet far enough advanced to be able to describe it. For to that which Eastern Theosophy calls Nirvana and which lies above the ' World of Providence,' one cannot just give any name one pleases.

As I was saying, between death and rebirth, man ascends to the higher Devachan or world of Reason. When there he looks into higher worlds, worlds he cannot himself enter, and there he sees the Higher Beings at work. Whereas man spends his life in worlds extending between the physical plane and Devachan, it is normal for the Bodhisattvas to extend to the Buddhi-plane, or what we in Europe call the world of Providence. That is a good name, for it is precisely the task of the Bodhisattvas to guide the world as a good ' providence ' from age to age. Now what took place when the Bodhisattva went through the embodiment of Gautama Buddha ?—When he reaches a certain stage, he can ascend to the next higher plane—to the Nirvana-Plane. That is his next sphere. It is characteristic of the Bodhisattvas that when they become Buddhas they ascend to the Plane of Nirvana. Everything that works on the inner being of man, dwells in a sphere extending to that Plane. A Being such as the Christ works into the nature of man from the other side. He also works, from the other side, into those worlds to which the Bodhisattvas ascend when they leave the region of man, in order themselves to learn, in order that they may become Teachers of humanity. There they meet,—coming down to them from above, from the other side—a Being such as the Christ. They then become pupils of Christ. A Being such as He, is surrounded by twelve Bodhisattvas ; we cannot indeed speak of more than twelve ; for when the twelve Bodhisattvas have accomplished their mission we shall have completed the period of earth-existence.

Christ was once on earth ; He has descended to earth, has dwelt on the earth, has ascended from it. He comes from the other side ; He is the Being who is in the midst of the twelve Bodhisattvas, and they receive from Him what they have to carry down to earth.—Thus, between two incarnations the Bodhisattva-Beings ascend to the Buddhi-Plane ; there they meet the Being of Christ as Teacher, and they are fully conscious of Him. He in this Being, extends to that Plane. The meeting between the Bodhisattvas and the Christ takes place on the Buddhi-Plane. When men progress further and shall have developed the qualities instilled into them by the Bodhisattvas, they will become more and more worthy themselves to penetrate that sphere. In the meantime it is necessary that they should learn that the Christ-Being was incarnated in human form in Jesus of Nazareth, and that in order to reach the true Being of the Individuality of Christ, one must first permeate the human form with understanding.

Thus twelve Bodhisattvas belong to Christ, and they prepare and further develop what He brought as the greatest impulse in the evolution of human civilisation. We see the twelve, and—in their midst—the thirteenth. We have now ascended to the sphere of the Bodhisattvas, and entered a circle of twelve stars ; in their midst is the Sun, illuminating, warming them ; from this Sun they draw that source of life which they afterwards have to carry down to earth.

How is the image of what takes place above, represented on earth ? It is projected into the earth in such wise that we may render it in the following words : Christ, Who once lived on the earth, brought to this earth evolution an impulse for which the Bodhisattvas had to prepare humanity and they then had to develop further what He gave to the earth-evolution. Thus the picture on earth, is something like this : Christ in the middle of the earth-evolution ; the Bodhisattvas as His advance-messengers and His followers, who have to bring His work closer to the minds and hearts of men.

A number of Bodhisattvas had thus to prepare mankind, to make men ripe to receive the Christ. Now, although men were ripe enough to have Christ among them, it will be a long time before they mature sufficiently to recognise, to feel, and to will, all that Christ is. The same number of Bodhisattvas will be required to develop to maturity in man what was poured into him through Christ, as was necessary to prepare men for His coming. For there is so much in Him, that the forces and faculties of men must go on ever increasing, before they are able to understand Him. With the existing faculties of man, Christ can only be understood to a minute extent. Higher faculties will arise in man, and each new faculty will enable him to see Christ in a new light. Only when the last Bodhisattva belonging to Christ shall have completed his work, will humanity realise what Christ really is ; man will then be filled with a will in which the Christ Himself will live. He will draw into man through his Thinking, Feeling, and Willing, and man will then really be the external expression of Christ on the earth.

LECTURE 2.

THE LAW OF KARMA WITH RESPECT TO THE DETAILS OF LIFE.

Berlin, 22nd December, 1909.

Our lecture to-day shall be devoted to subjects interesting to Anthroposophists in the widest sense, subjects intended to throw light on certain points which may have puzzled those who have attended our Group-Meetings for a considerable time. It is well, now and then, to recollect that the point of importance in Anthroposophy is not so much the learning of certain things as theory or doctrine, but that we should continually enter in greater detail into the questions and enigmas of life.—Some people may perhaps say : ' All that is necessary to know of Anthroposophy for use in life could be comfortably contained in a small pamphlet of sixty pages or so ; everyone could possess a copy and would then be convinced as to the nature of man, reincarnation and karma, and the evolution of humanity on the earth,—and could go through life needing nothing further.' A person who would like to have that carried out might perhaps suggest : ' Why does not the Anthroposophical Movement distribute as many copies as possible of a booklet containing these principal points of view, so that everyone might acquire a copy and be able to convince himself ? Why does the Anthroposophical Society adopt the curious method of holding meetings week after week, assembling all those interested or likely to become interested for the purpose of constantly recapitulating what might comfortably be reduced to a sixty-page pamphlet ? What can these Anthroposophists possibly have to say to their followers, week after week ? '

There may be certain orders of mind of our day who would like to have a small outline of Anthroposophy which they could keep in their waistcoat pockets, and thus study what it is most important to know. We must, however, over and over again, bring to mind the fact that nothing can be done in this way with Anthroposophy. There can be no ' tabloid-knowledge ! ' Although Anthroposophy does depend both on knowledge and perception, it does not consist of mere ' phrases,' but of very definite knowledge. But it is not enough merely to acquire this knowledge as a general conviction according to present-day methods, and then rest satisfied. For the point in question is not merely that one should acquire the conviction and know that man lives many lives and that there are causal conditions which pass over from one life into another, that there is such a thing as reincarnation, as karma. The beneficial effects of Anthroposophy do not lie in the spreading of this knowledge, but are felt in the constant and repeated study of all the details connected with it, and in allowing the teaching to work upon one's soul. It does one no good simply to believe that man lives more than once and that there is such a law as that of reincarnation, karma, and so on. The mere belief in this will not carry one far. As regards the real depths of life there is not much difference between the soul of a man who knows of reincarnation and karma and one who knows nothing of it. In an anthroposophical sense our soul is only changed if we constantly study, not only the generalities, but the deeper things that Spiritual Science can teach us. That is why it is a good thing that we should over and over again consider how the various details of life appear in the light of the Anthroposophical conception. It is by no means sufficient merely to know that there is a great law of destiny establishing a connection between the past deeds, feelings and thoughts of a man and his present and future experiences. Anthroposophy will only become a life-factor when we can apply this general doctrine to the different experiences of life, when we become able to put our whole soul into such a position, that we obtain an entirely new outlook on life. That is why we will to-day give a little time to studying the law of karma, the great law of destiny, with reference to the details of life. Things will be spoken of to-day which are familiar to all ; but they will be considered from the standpoint of karma.

Karma says in a general sense that there is a connection in the spiritual world between what takes place to-day and what has taken place in the past. It is not really a good thing to call karma the law of causality, and then to compare it with the law of cause and effect in the external world. If we wish to find a comparison for this great law of destiny, we must take care that the comparison is valid, that it really does represent this law.

Let us take the following as an example. Suppose we have two vessels containing water—and two metal balls of the normal temperature of the living-room. We throw one ball into one of the vessels ; and the water remains as it was. We now take the other ball and having heated it, we throw it into the other vessel. The water in that gets warm.—Why has the water in the second vessel grown warm and not in the first ? Because the ball itself underwent a change before it was thrown into the vessel ; and having itself been made hot it brings about the warming of the water. An event occurred which was the result of another event, the result of the ball having been heated.—The experiences and activities of a former time are connected with the experiences and phenomena of the present or future.

When we grasp the law of the spiritual connections between past, present and future in this way, we shall be able to find it confirmed in ordinary life, in the everyday life around us,—though we ourselves may be very far from having as yet developed any clairvoyant faculties. For we must always establish as a golden rule the fact that while a law of the spiritual world can only be proved by the spiritual investigator through clairvoyant observation, it can always be corroborated by the experiences of the external world.—People will, however, have to accustom themselves to observe external life a little more carefully than usual, if they wish to find confirmation of the law of karma. As a rule they do not see, figuratively speaking, beyond ' the end of their noses.' What lies beyond that, they do not observe. Anyone who observes more profoundly will, however, find plenty of confirmation between birth and death of the existence of a law of karma.   We will keep as far as possible to the concrete, and take the following example.   A young lad, fifteen years of age, has been torn away by unforeseen circumstances from the life he had been accustomed to lead.   Till then the position of his parents had permitted him to study ; now at the age of fifteen, in consequence, perhaps, of his father having lost his fortune, he had to go into trade, and was thus pitchforked from one calling to another. Of course the point here is not that the one calling was in any way better than the other, but that his life was altered by the change.   Now people who contemplate life in the ordinary materialistic sense would probably not expect anything worthy of note to be brought about by the influence of such an event in a man's life, and they would find nothing.   But a closer observer would discover that a young man who goes into trade in that way, will at first feel pleasure in the change, will like his calling,—that his interest in it grows with his own growth, as one might say.   After a while, however, something remarkable will become evident.   The soul-experiences, the sympathies and antipathies he feels in his work, may, as he reaches the age of eighteen or nineteen, assume a different form.   He may cease to take pleasure in it ; his attitude towards trade may alter.   Those who had never heard of Anthroposophy would feel at a loss to account for what takes place in the young man's soul.

What then has actually occurred ?—When the young man was fifteen and was put into the new trade, he took a great interest in it.   At first the interest he felt drove out the feelings and sentiments that had formed within him when he was following a different line of activity.   Those feelings were pushed into the background.   The time, however, comes when these break through again with all the more strength.   It is just as though one compressed an elastic object ; it can be compressed for a while but it springs back with all the more rapidity, and the result in the case of the lad may be that the interests which have been thrust aside for a time, now burst forth with greater zest.   When he is eighteen or nineteen the feelings and sentiments that penetrated his soul, three years before the change of calling, now come forth anew,—that is, those he felt at eleven or twelve.—Life can only be explained in such a case by saying : When this lad was fifteen a turning-point occurred in his life.   After that, things happened whose external effects are felt the same number of years after the turning-point as the cause of them originated before that time.

Just think how one would be able to help a person as regards his soul-moods and the difficulties of life, if we were able to ask ourselves :—When did such a turning-point occur ?—It may have been connected with something quite private and intimate ; but, if one can place it, we can then reckon back ; and it will be found that the spiritual effects reveal themselves just as long after the turning-point, as the cause of them was before that time.   This gives one an insight into karma.   Such knowledge is a help in life, and we may say :— Causes and effects of this nature are connected with definite periods of time and they are determined by a definite period in life, so that if we count backwards and forwards from that point of time, we can find the connection between cause and effect.

Now this might, of course, be concealed by the intervention of other events. Someone might say : ' The example you have just given us is no use ; I have just met a young man to whom it does not apply : '—Well,—I have known a case of two men having a game of billiards, when a passing waiter bumped into the one who was just about to play, thus driving his ball in quite a different direction from what was intended ! The law of cause and effect was not at fault, but other circumstances intervened. We must reflect that we shall never learn to know that law if we do not make an exception of the things that upset it. After the age of fifteen other circumstances may arise which interfere with the law. We do not become acquainted with laws simply by observing life, but by acquiring the right method of summing up its phenomena. For in life things are being constantly disturbed and the laws cannot so easily be seen ; we can only regulate our life by knowing how these laws are to be found. When we know the particulars, we can say in the case of the young man whose life has been so smashed up, that it is the task of those who have his education in hand to look out for the result. In this way karma becomes a law of life ; and if we have knowledge of the law, we can make use of our knowledge when such a case occurs. If we find that we can no longer give the lad what he had before, we can at any rate become his adviser. But we can only give the right advice if we know of the existence of such connections as those I have spoken of,—if we know what is the matter with him and intervene with help just where and when his particular lack is making itself felt. If we are ignorant of this law we cannot help him with advice.—When we regard the law of karma as a law of life it may become an influence in life, we can learn to become counsellors.

The above-mentioned case does not of course exhaust all the combinations that are possible ; there is another way in which the law of karma is experienced between birth and death. There is a remarkable connection between the experiences a man has in the first half of his life and the second,—but this is not as a rule observed. One often makes acquaintance with a man in his youth and loses sight of him before he reaches maturity ; or else one only meets a man when he is already old and one knows nothing of his youth ; or even if one did know him in youth, one may have forgotten what has happened to him since. Were we to study and compare the beginning and end of people's lives when it is possible so to do, we should find the finest confirmation of the law of karma even in the life between birth and death.

Perhaps you may remember in this connection what I have said in public lectures about the ' noble ' anger which appears in youth. I have explained that a young person is not able fully to judge of an injustice that may be going on in his vicinity ; he is not yet mature enough. Yet the wise rulership of the world has so ordained things that our feelings will help us to judge truly before our reason is mature enough to do so. A noble nature will, even in childhood, be moved to a righteous anger by anything like injustice, although it may be only in his feeling that his soul can sense the injustice. He may perhaps not yet be ripe to judge of it through his intellect. When this noble sense of indignation is to be found in the character of a child we ought to take particular note of it, for the feeling aroused by the injustice remains in the soul. This noble anger in early youth permeates the soul and, as life goes on, it becomes transformed. In the second half of life it reapppears in a different form ; it appears as the quality of loving kindness and goodness. We shall not often find that loving, bounteous goodness in the latter part of a man's life—if other things are equal and nothing has occurred to distort the sequence—without finding that it was expressed in his early years by a noble anger aroused at the stupidity or the ugly things of life.   In ordinary life we find a karmic connection which we may clothe in the form of a picture and say : The hand that never clenched its fist in noble anger in the first half of life, will not easily be stretched forth in blessing in the latter half.—Such things will of course only be observed by one who can see a little further than ' the end of his nose,' which is just what most people do not do.   I might give a simple example to show how little people are inclined to notice such things in life.

I have often mentioned how helpful it is to one who wishes to become intimately acquainted with life in order to study more deeply the occult conditions of the soul, to have been a teacher at some time.   One learns more of the soul in that way than can be learnt from the ordinary text-books on Psychology, which, as a rule, are quite valueless.   A knowledge of the soul is acquired when we do not merely observe and study but have to take the responsibility of guiding and directing the life of others.   One learns a closer observation. During the long years of my tutorship I not only observed the children of whom I had charge, but I had many opportunities when other families came to visit them, of studying other children of all ages, even from the time they came into the world.

That is now some twenty-five to thirty years ago.   You may have noticed how every five years or thereabouts the doctors have a different opinion as to what is ' good ' for people.   Well,—at that time they were strongly of opinion that it was very strengthening for delicate children three, four or five years old, to drink a glass of red wine every day.—I knew certain children who had their glass of wine and others who did not, and was able to make my own observations. For of course at that time, the doctor's opinion was considered infallible.   It would have been of no use to attempt to go against it.   I was thus able to await results.   The children who were then from two to five years old and who were given the glass of wine to strengthen them, are now young men and women of twenty-five to twenty-eight years of age.   I particularly noticed that only then the results of this treatment show themselves.   All the children who had the wine have become ' Fidgety Phils '; their astral bodies are fidgety, they have not much control of them ; they do not know how to control the involuntary movements of their soul-life.   On the other hand, those children who,—unfortunately, as was then said,—could not have their glass of red wine, have now become stable natures, less ' wobbly ' in their astral bodies, or, as materialists would say, in their nervous systems.

This is an example of the connections that exist in life.   It is rather a trivial one and not particularly illustrative of karma ; but it serves to show that we should not only look as far as the end of our noses but should survey longer periods of time, and that it is not sufficient merely to affirm that a remedy will have such and such an effect, for what is actually brought about can only be observed by the true observer many years after.   Nothing but the great connections and all that leads us to find them can in reality give us the true explanations of the relation between cause and effect in the life of man.   Thus we must try to connect the qualities of the soul with those phenomena of life which lie apparently very far apart ; and we shall then be able to trace the law of karma even between birth and death, and shall frequently find that the events of later life are connected with the experiences of the earlier.

You may remember what I said of the mission of Devotion, of the importance of looking up in feeling to some being or some phenomenon which we do not yet understand, but which we revere for the very reason that we have not yet grown up to the level of being able to understand it. I always like to remind you of how fortunate it is when a man can say : 'As a child I heard of a member of our family who was very greatly respected and honoured. I had not yet seen him but I had a profound reverence for him. Then one day the opportunity came, and I was taken to see him. A feeling of profound and holy awe came over me as I laid my hand on the handle of the door of the room where this wonderful person was to be seen.'

In later life a man will have good reason to be grateful for that feeling of reverent devotion ; we owe much gratitude to anyone who aroused a feeling of reverence in us in our early life. That feeling is of great and special value in any life. I have known men who exclaim, when such a feeling of reverent devotion to the Spiritual and Divine is alluded to : ' I am an Atheist ! I cannot revere anything spiritual ! '—We can reply : ' Look at the starry heavens ! Could you create those ? Look at that wisdom-filled structure and reflect : there it is surely possible to have a feeling of real, true reverence.' There are many things in the world which our understanding has not yet grown up to, but to which we can look up in reverence. Especially is this the case in youth, when there is so much we can look up to and venerate, without being able to understand it.

A feeling of devotion in early youth is transformed into a very special quality in the second half of life. We have all heard of persons who just by being themselves, are, as it were, a blessing to those around them. There is no need for them to say anything particular, their presence is enough. It seems as though by the very nature of their being, something invisible flows forth from them to the souls around them. Through their very nature they radiate a healing and beneficent influence on their environment. To what do these people owe their power of blessing ? They owe it to the circumstance that in their youth they lived a life in which reverence played a part. Reverence in the early part of their life was transformed in later years into a force which works invisibly, pouring forth blessing and help. Here again is a karmic connection which, if we look for it, is clearly and distinctly to be observed. It was really a true feeling for karma which led Goethe to choose as the motto for one of his works, these beautiful words : ' What we desire in our youth is fulfilled in old age ! ' If one only observes the connections to be found within short periods of time, it may certainly seem as though one could speak of unfulfilled wishes,—but taking longer spans of time, this cannot well be said. All these things can pass over into and become part of life's daily round ; and as a matter of fact, only one who studies in this anthroposophical way is qualified to educate children, for he will be able to provide them in their early years with that which, as he knows, they will be able to use in the latter part of their life. The responsibility that a man assumes when he instils one thing or another into a child is not realised to-day. It has become the custom to look down on these things to-day—to speak of them from the high horse of materialistic thinking. I should like to illustrate this by an experience we ourselves once had here in Berlin.

A theosophical visitor once came here,—one of those who think if at some time in their lives they have attended one or two meetings, they are well able to form an opinion on the whole subject. Such persons desire to learn about a spiritual Movement like Anthroposophy so as to be able to write objectively about it. Those who wish to provide the world with newspaper articles, believe that they can judge of a movement by going to one or two lectures !—This visitor also went away and wrote. It was curious to read later on in an American paper what was said of one of our anthroposophical meetings. Of course the description given was remarkably correct !—As I have said, if anyone really wishes to grasp Anthroposophy it cannot be done in that way ; it is only possible to penetrate into the life of Anthroposophy if one has the distinct will really to enter into it in detail and experience. I am only saying all this to characterise the opinion formed by this visitor, which he did not hide under a bushel ! He said he did not like the way in which Anthroposophy splits up everything,—dividing the world into physical world, astral world, devachanic world, and so on. Why should everything be so split up ?—This was after one or two visits. What a terrible effect it would have had on him if he had heard of the other divisions ! He was of the opinion that it was unnecessary to consider things in this way, but that one should speak of the spiritual world in general terms.—Why should it be divided into classes ?

That is the way people talk to-day about Education and all other departments of life ; Science itself talks in the same way. The world talks from an arbitrary observation of life, not from an objective investigation of the separate phenonomena. That is why the impressions which all such reforms and programmes must make on one who is able really to observe the world is so dreadful ; they arouse a feeling that may be compared to physical pain. Take any ordinary book on Science to-day ; no matter how conscientiously the conclusions are drawn, it is terrible to see how they are put forward, for there is no conception of the way the phenomena ought to be observed. In the same way many a man is admired to-day, who blazens forth his opinion, based simply on his own predelictions or antipathies.

It is of immense importance that Anthroposophy should become aware of the fact that life must be observed, down to its very smallest details, according to the methods which the knowledge of karma and other laws put into our hands. That is why we can only hope for a blessing on the future evolution of humanity—even as regards the question of Education—if the anthroposophical views penetrate to the fundamental principles of Education. Karma provides a firm support for all questions connected with that.

For instance, it is extremely important that we should know the karmic connections of a certain phenomenon in Education expressed in the view : ' If a child is properly brought up, he must be this or that—that is what I admire ! ' It seems as though the child were supposed to be a sack, into which one can stuff whatever is thought to be right! People wish to stamp their own nature, with its personal sympathies or antipathies, upon the child. If they knew the karmic consequences of this, they would take a different view. They would see that what is stuffed in that way into a child, as into a sack, will work out karmically by making the grown man or woman a hard, dry nature, prematurely old, for the very core of their being is killed. If we wish to educate a child, and to imbue it with any particular quality, we must set to work in a roundabout way. We must not try to force it upon the child, rather ought we to arouse a longing for that particular quality, so that the child itself will desire to acquire it. We must even go a step further. If we know that a particular food is good for a child we must not force him to eat it, but should try so to cultivate his taste, that he will ask for it of his own accord. That is a very different method to that of forcing everything into him as into a sack, saying :— ' in with you ! '—If we begin to regulate the child's requirements, we reach the very life-germ of his being and we shall see the effects of this working out karmically in the second half of his life, in his joy in life, in his life-force. In his later years, instead of being arid and dry, he will remain alive in the centre of his being.

If we consider the law of karma in this way we shall say : ' It does not suffice merely to write a little book entitled ' There is a law of karma, a connection between the earlier and the later,' but we must study life itself in the light of that law. Anthroposophy is only present in its true form when we enter into all the details of life ; but we must also determine to do this work without cessation. We must find time to study all the phenomena of life from the standpoint of Anthroposophy.

The above are a few of the things that indicate the connections to be found in life between birth and death. Now we can follow out the law of karma beyond this limit and connect one life with other lives or with one other. We must connect what we experience to-day, in the present life between birth and death, with things we experienced formerly, or that we shall experience later, in subsequent lives. I will to-day confine myself to throwing light on one important question, from the standpoint of karma in so far as it extends from one life into another. That is, the question of health and sickness, more especially the latter.

Many people when they are stricken with some malady, believe that according to karma they would be right in supposing they have brought it upon themselves, that it is their fate ; but that alone does not always characterise karma aright. Where there is a malady we must first of all be quite clear as to the nature of the trouble in a spiritual sense. It will be well to begin with the nature of pain, and then pass on to the spiritual understanding of the nature of illness.

What is the nature of pain ? We will now consider external pain, such, for instance, as we feel when we cut our finger. Why does that hurt ?—We shall never be able to explain the nature of pain from the spiritual standpoint if we do not realise that the physical finger is permeated by an etheric and an astral finger. The outward appearance of the physical finger, its shape, the way in which the blood circulates in it and the position of the nerves within it,—all these things are determined by the etheric finger. It is the builder ; and still takes care that the nerves are in their proper place and that the blood flows in the right way. The way in which the etheric body carries out these functions is regulated by the astral body, which permeates the whole. We will now explain by an external example why it hurts when we cut a finger.

Perhaps it may be a favourite occupation of yours to water the flowers in your garden once a day ; that gives you a feeling of satisfaction. One morning, however, you find that your watering-pot is spoilt or perhaps stolen, and you are not able to water your garden. You are distressed ; what you feel is not physical pain, yet the fact that you are prevented from carrying out your favourite occupation may somewhat resemble that ; you cannot carry out an activity because you lack the necessary instrument. The external lack felt in this instance, which can only call forth a moral pain, may become a physical pain in the way that will now be described.

The etheric and astral bodies are organised for the purpose of maintaining the finger as it now is. I can never cut the etheric finger nor the astral finger. If I cut my finger in two, the etheric finger can no longer carry out its proper duty. It is accustomed to have the fingers in their right connection. Now this connection is interrupted :—just as your activity was interrupted, when you wanted to water your garden. Thus the astral and etheric bodies are not able to intervene, and the prevention from exercising the usual activity is felt in the astral body as pain. But the moment these bodies are interrupted, they make an extra effort,—just as you, wishing to water your garden, would make extra efforts to find the watering-pot or the like. In the same way our astral and etheric bodies must now call forth greater activity in order to repair the injury. It is the extra activity thus called forth which is the actual healing force. Whatever calls forth great activity in the spiritual bodies of man, produces healing. Now the cause of all illness is, that through some disorder in the physical or even in the etheric body of man, the spiritual principles are prevented from intervening in the proper way, they are hindered, as it were ; and the healing consists in the calling forth of a stronger resistance to the disorder.—An illness may either be healed, or we may die of it.—Let us consider both these possibilities from the karmic standpoint.

If the illness takes such a course that we recover from it, it means that in those members that we have brought with us from former incarnations, we had stored up such strong life-force that it is able to intervene and heal us. When we look back at those incarnations we can say :—Not only were we able at the time to provide for what we normally have in life, but we brought with us a reserve fund, which we may call up from the spiritual members of our life.

Now, suppose we die. How does the case stand then ?—We must then say : ' When the effort to heal was made, we called upon the strongest forces within us—but they did not suffice. Yet whenever we call up these forces, demanding extra strength from them, it is not without avail, for in so doing we have had to make stronger efforts. Although we may not be able in this life to restore order to any one part of our organism, yet it has, none the less, grown stronger. We desired to resist the malady, but our powers did not suffice. Yet although they did not succeed, the forces we called up in making

23

the effort, are not lost. They pass over into the next incarnation and the injured organ will then be stronger than if we had not had the disturbance. We are then able to build up the particular organ that brought us a premature death and to impart to it special strength and regularity. This will be all the more successfully accomplished if we treat the illness in the right way and yet are not able to cure it. In such a case we must look upon the illness, karmically, as something which will in a future life prove to have been fortunate. We shall then have gained a special strength through having fought the malady though we were unable to cure it.—One ought not, however, on that account, to say : ' Perhaps it might be as well to let an illness take its course, for then if we do not interfere and try to curb it, the forces within us will be stronger and our karma will have a better fulfilment.—That would be nonsense. The point is this : the healing must be carried out in such a way that the equalising forces are able to intervene in as favourable a manner as possible ; in other words, we must do all in our power to bring about a cure, regardless of whether it be successful or not. Karma is always a friend, never an enemy to life !

By this example it is proved that the law of karma, which extends from one life to another, works for the strengthening of life. We can, therefore, say that if any one organ is particularly strong, this points to a preceding life in which that organ was once ailing and we were not able to heal it. The forces for so doing were called up and they have caused it to grow particularly strong now. Thus we see the events and facts stretching across from one life into another. If we become conscious in the right way of how it can be strengthened, our life-kernel will become stronger and stronger. In this way we can attain a more and more living comprehension of our spiritual life-kernel through the law of karma.

We now come to an answer to the question : ' Why do we meet together so often ? ' We do so, because not only do we enrich our knowledge when we take in anthroposophical teaching, but also because, if it be given in the right way, it is able to make our life-kernel more and more strong and forceful. We pour a spiritual life-sap into all we do, by meeting together and occupying ourselves with Anthroposophy. Thus Anthroposophy is not a theory, it is a life-giving draught, an elixir of life which ever anew pours itself into our souls and of which we know that it will make them grow stronger and stronger. When Anthroposophy emerges from the position which now, through lack of comprehension, it occupies in the outer world, when it really intervenes in our whole spiritual life, people will then see how the salvation, even of the physical life, of the purely external life, will depend on the strengthening which can be acquired through the study of Anthroposophy. The time will come when anthroposophical gatherings will be the most important sources of strength to man, from which they will go forth, saying : we are most grateful to these meetings, for we owe to them our health and strength and the fact that we are constantly able to strengthen anew our own life-kernel, the core of our being. People will only realise what the mission of Anthroposophy is, when they feel that it furnishes us with the means of working forcefully on the physical body and making it sound and healthy. Those who are occupying themselves with Anthroposophy to-day, should regard themselves as pioneers for Anthroposophy as a means of strengthening life. Then only will it become what it ought to be, the right point of attack against something which in many cases is weakening life to-day.

In conclusion I will draw your attention to one thing more. There is no phrase more frequently mentioned than 'inherited tendency.' No man is considered an educated man to-day who does not mention it at least two or three times a week! An educated man must at least make himself acquainted with what the learned medical profession has ascertained as to 'inherited tendencies.' When a person does not know what to make of himself, most people say at once : ' he is suffering from an inherited tendency.' Anyone not saying that is regarded as badly educated, perhaps among other things an Anthroposophist!—Here Science begins not only to go astray in theory, but also to be injurious to life. This is the boundary where theory encroaches on morality—where it is immoral to hold a wrong theory. Here life's strength and security really depend on correct knowledge. What will a man be able to do who, through the right spiritual conception in his soul, strengthens, fortifies himself by taking in the elixir of life ? No matter what he may have inherited, these inheritances are only in the physical body or at most in the etheric body. Through his right conception of the world he will be able to make his own vital centre stronger and stronger, and will be able to conquer his inherited tendencies ; for the spiritual, if present in the right way, is able to equalise the body. If, however, a man does not strengthen the spiritual core of his being, merely asserting that the spiritual is the fruit of the physical, he will have a weak inner nature, he will be the victim of his inherited tendencies ; they will work harmfully in him. No wonder then, that so-called inherited tendencies have such dreadful results ; for people are first of all talked into belief of the powers of such tendencies and are deprived of what counteracts them. The belief in inherited tendencies is cultivated, and the spiritual conception of the world,— the best weapon with which to fight them,—is taken away. First the power of the inherited tendencies is discovered, and by this means they become active. Not only is this a wrong insight, which arouses a life-destroying activity and takes the weapons of defence out of the hands of the sufferer, but it is the beginning of a theory based absolutely on a materialistic conception. Here a materialistic conception of the world begins to play a part which is in effect not only theoretically incorrect but immoral.—This cannot be got over, simply by saying that those who assert such things are mistaken. We need not be too severe in judging those who put forth these theories. We are not attacking individual scientists here ; it is quite comprehensible that they are involved in a line of thought which must lead to such errors—we must admit this in all fairness. The one, perhaps, may not be able to free himself from scientific tradition ; another perhaps considers it excusable, for, having a wife and children he would be in an awkward position if he were to break away from the ruling opinions. But the whole thing must be considered as a phenomenon of the times, for Science is beginning not only to spread abroad false theories, but to take away the life-promoting remedies, the spiritual conception of life, which is able to fortify and which is alone able to stand up against the physical, —the power which must otherwise overwhelm man. The physical can only possess overwhelming power as long as a man does not build up strength in his spiritual nature. If he does this, a warrior will grow up within him, a warrior who will defend him against the physical.

We cannot hope that this should come about from one day to the next. But those who have the right understanding of things will gradually learn the anthroposophical view of phenomena in face of which man at first seems power-less. What is not equalised in one life is made good in the long run. If we contemplate a single life, as well as life from incarnation to incarnation, we shall see that rightly understood, karma is a law that no longer depresses us, but rather one which brings us comfort and force whereby to make ourselves stronger. The law of karma is a law of life, and we must understand it as such. The point is, not that we should know a few single abstract thoughts, but that we should study the life-truths of Anthroposophy in the details of life, and never weary of anthroposophical work, while we permeate ourselves with its different truths.

If you hold this as an ideal before you, you will be living an anthroposo-phical life in the true sense of the words. You will then know why it is that we do not satisfy ourselves with merely reading one or two books, but regard Anthroposophy as something in which our heart is concerned and which never ceases to occupy us ; something to which we gladly return again and again, and of which we know that the oftener we return the more it will enrich our lives.

LECTURE 3.

THE ENTRANCE OF THE CHRIST-BEING INTO THE EVOLUTION OF HUMANITY.

Berlin, 2nd February, 1910.

In each of the Gospels light is thrown on the great Mystery of Golgotha from one particular aspect. I have drawn your attention to the fact that the secret of Golgotha, the secret of Christ Jesus, is presented by the Gospel of St. Mark from the aspect of the great Cosmological connections, while that of St. Matthew shows how this secret was developed out of one special people, the ancient Hebrews. We have seen how that people had to develop little by little, from generation to generation, from the time of Abraham, so as to bring forth later, as their flower, the Human Being in whom could be contained the individuality of Zarathustra or Zoroaster. We have seen how all the qualities peculiar to the Hebrew people,—qualities which had to become more and more intensified in the course of their descent from one generation to the next—were based entirely on the principle of physical inheritance. We were thus able to describe how the character of the mission of the old Hebrew people differed from that of others in that it had to inherit certain qualities, which could only be attained by physical inheritance, and which had gained in intensity from the oldest generations of the time of Abraham down to Jesus. The Gospel of St. Matthew contains many other secrets, as indeed do all the Gospels. Although in the course of this Winter we shall open up a few aspects and perspective glimpses into the Gospels, these can at the most only stimulate the understanding. For in order to understand the Gospels completely a never-ending spiritual work is necessary. Light shall be thrown to-day from one particular side on the Gospel of St. Matthew and it will be shown how the lessons to be drawn therefrom can be usefully applied by those who now form part of the anthroposophical spiritual stream.

If we look back at much of what we have learnt as the years went by, we shall see that the development of humanity, as described by Spiritual Science, passes through various crises ; it reaches an important point, then continues for a while along a more level road, then comes another important point, and so on. We have often emphasised that one such important point in the development of humanity on earth was reached when the Christ-Impulse was given at the beginning of our era, according to the modern reckoning of time. When we look back beyond the Atlantean into the Lemurian age, we come to that point in time when the first rudiment of the human ego was implanted in

27

the human being. To understand such an event, the words must be taken very accurately. For instance, we must make a clear distinction between the statement that in the Lemurian epoch 'the first rudiments of the ego were implanted in the human being,' and that other, that 'at the time of the Mystery of Golgotha began the period, the age, in which humanity became conscious of this ego.' There is a great difference between having the ego only in rudiment, as something working in man, and the knowledge that one possesses it. A sharp distinction must be made between these things, for otherwise it is impossible to understand the true laws of evolution.

We know that the implanting of the ego in man is part of the collective development of the earth. The earth passed through the Saturn, Sun and Moon ages, and then only did it become the structure it is to-day. On Saturn the germ of the physical body was laid, on the Sun that of the etheric body, on the Moon that of the astral body, and the germ of the ego was added on the earth; this germ was placed in the development of the earth in the Lemurian epoch. Now something else also took place in the Lemurian epoch, something that we have always called 'the luciferic influence.' During that epoch man was endowed with the germ of the ego, which in the course of the subsequent earth-periods was destined to attain greater and greater perfection, and at the same time his astral body was 'inoculated' with the luciferic influence. The whole nature of man was altered by this influence, even to the forces and elements in his etheric and physical bodies. Thus in the Lemurian epoch man became an entirely different being from what he would have been if there had been no luciferic influence. We see him altering in two respects: we see him becoming an ego-being—and we see him becoming a being in whom the luciferic principle is hidden. Even if the luciferic principle had not set in, the ego-influence would still have entered man.

Now what took place in the human being as a result of the luciferic influence having made itself felt in the Lemurian epoch?

When such a circumstance is described from one aspect or another, I beg you not to consider that as all that can be said on the subject; for this may well be only one point of view, selected for the moment. In the course of years a great deal has been said as to what the luciferic influence brought about in the evolution of man; it is all part of the same, but we cannot repeat it all now. To-day we will select one point of view only, that describes one aspect; that is, that as a result of the luciferic influence man reached a certain point in evolution earlier than was intended, earlier than the wise guidance of the world had predestined for him. The luciferic influence caused him to descend more deeply into the three principles which came over from the former embodiments of the earth, (the astral body, etheric body and physical body) and he has become more entangled in them than would have been the case if no such influence had prevailed. Man, with his ego, would have remained nearer to the spiritual worlds, he would have continued for a longer time to feel himself, through his ego, a member of the spiritual world, if the luciferic influence had not caused that ego to descend more deeply into the three principles. We may say that as a result of the luciferic influence, man descended more deeply on to the earth in the Lemurian epoch. We can indicate the time when he would have descended thus far to the earth or into physical matter had there been no luciferic influence ; it would have been in the middle of the Atlantean epoch. If no luciferic influence had come about man would have been obliged to wait till then for his descent to earth ; but that influence caused him to descend earlier. It enabled him to become a free being, able to act in accordance with his own impulses. He would otherwise have remained entirely dependent upon the spiritual world until the middle of the Atlantis epoch ; neither would he have been able before then to distinguish between good and evil, nor act from his own impulses. He could only have acted from psychic influences, that is to say, from forces implanted in his soul by Divine Spiritual Beings. The luciferic beings made it possible for him to begin at an earlier stage to decide between good and evil ; not simply to allow himself to be guided by the laws of the divine-spiritual world Order, but to decide for himself, creating a kind of law and order for himself. This fact is expressed in a very profound way in the description of ' the Fall,' which represents in a wonderful imaginative picture, what I have just stated. The Old Testament describes this by saying that Divine Spiritual Beings implanted into man ' a living soul.' Now if this living soul had merely remained as it was, man would have had to wait until later on, until the Divine Spiritual Beings had brought the living soul, or, in other words, the yet undeveloped ego, to the degree of maturity able to make distinctions. But now there came the luciferic influences, represented in the Bible as ' the Serpent.' Through these, man himself became able to distinguish between good and evil, instead of merely instinctively following the inpourings of Jehovah or the Elohim. From a being who till that time had been guided and led by Divine Spiritual Beings, man thus became a being able to decide for himself. The Bible clearly shows that self-decision was brought to man by the Serpent, or in other words, by the luciferic beings. We then hear the words ring forth, words spoken from the side of the gods : ' Man has become as one of us ! ' Or, if we wish to put this into plainer words :—' Man has acquired something through the luciferic influence which has till now been reserved only for the gods. It was given to the gods to decide between good and evil, the beings dependent upon them had no such decisions to make.'

As a result of the luciferic influence man now became a being capable of making distinctions ; that is, he became a being who developed divine qualities within him prematurely. In this way and through this influence, something entered human nature which would otherwise have been withheld from his evolution till the middle of the Atlantean epoch. As you can well imagine, man would have been quite different if this descent into matter had not taken place till then ; his soul would have been more mature for the descent. He would have descended into matter as a better, a riper, man. He would have brought quite different qualities into his physical, etheric and astral bodies and would have possessed a very different power of distinguishing between good and evil. Because man was already a being able to distinguish between good and evil from the Lemurian epoch to the middle of the Atlantean epoch, he made himself worse than he would otherwise have been ; he entered a state of lesser perfection. He would otherwise have spent all the intervening time in a much more spiritual way ; but as it was, he passed through it more materially. The effect of this was that if he had received in the middle of the Atlantean epoch what the gods had intended him to have, he would have fallen utterly and completely.

What was it that would have been given to man at the middle of the Atlantean epoch, if he had continued to be guided and directed till that time, instinctively, as it were, by Divine Spiritual Beings?

He would have then received that which, the luciferic influence having in the meanwhile intervened, was afterwards given to him through the Mystery of Golgotha. The Christ-Impulse would have been given to man at the middle of the Atlantean epoch. Now, however, on account of the luciferic influence, man had to wait as long a time for the Christ-Impulse as had elapsed between the intervention of the luciferic influence and the middle of the Atlantean epoch. There was the same span of time between the entrance of Lucifer and the middle of the Atlantean epoch, as between that time and the arrival of the Christ-Impulse. Thus, through man's having acquired a likeness to the gods before he was meant to do so, we have to describe a delay of the Christ-Impulse. For before that could come man had to go through the Earth-Karma due to him on account of the evil that had entered the earth through the luciferic impulse. He had to wait, not only till that influence had rendered him able to distinguish between good and evil, but until, in the course of the earth's development, all the consequences of the luciferic influence had come. He had to wait for these, for then only could the Christ-Impulse descend to the earth. In accordance with the wise guidance of the earth, man was not intended to escape for ever from what was to come to him through the luciferic influence, but it would not have come upon him till the middle of the Atlantean epoch. It must have come in any case; but it would certainly not have come in the same form. Not only did man acquire from Lucifer the power of free decision in everything connected with spiritual things, but also the capacity of enthusiasm for what is good and noble, wise and great. As human beings, we are not only able coldly to distinguish between good and evil, but also to feel a warm glow for the noble, good and wise. That is because something was carried into our astral body, which, if it had only reached man in the middle of the Atlantean epoch, would have been taken into the ego, that ego which is capable of judgment. All the feeling, the idealism and enthusiasm for what is good, for high ideals, we owe to the circumstance that something entered our astral body before we had acquired the likeness to God in our ego, before the acceptance of the Christ had taken place therein. The essential point is that this likeness to God, the possibility of finding the good within ourselves, had to come to man. If the luciferic influence had not come, this impulse would have come in the middle of the Atlantean period, but as things are it came in the age in which Christ Jesus Himself worked.

Thus through the Christ-Impulse the consciousness came to man that in his ego he had something of Divine substance and of Divine nature. The thought that man can take in the Divine in his Ego-being and that this Divine part can be active therein and distinguish between good and evil, underlies all the deeper sayings of the New Testament. We may therefore say that with the reception into the inner nature of man of the Christ-Impulse, it was made

30

possible for man to say : 'I must be my own guide for the knowledge of my existence and the distinction between good and evil.'

Now if we look back to the pre-Christian time, we must say that when the impulse enabling man to distinguish between good and evil was not yet present, such distinction, and the judgment of man as to the good, the beautiful and the true, was necessarily meagre ; it did not actually proceed from his inner being. He could not, before the Christ-Impulse, have distinguished in his inner being between good and evil. In the pre-Christian time the decision as to the really Good, Beautiful and True could only be accomplished through certain beings— such as the Bodhisattvas—reaching up as time went on with a part of their being into the divine-spiritual worlds ; the distinction between good and evil was therefore not made from out of man's inner being, but in the divine worlds. Through their companionship with divine spiritual beings these Guides acquired it and it flowed from them into the souls of men, as though by suggestion. Had it not been for those guides, men could only have made feeble distinctions be- tween good and evil in those days. If these guides had depended on their own hearts alone, they could not have done this either ; but because they descended into those depths of the soul which were not yet accessible to man and entered in their ego-being into the kingdoms of heaven, they received the impulse needed by man to help him to decide between good and evil at the time of his need, that the good might nevertheless be implanted in the earth by way of preparation. Thus, before the time of Christ, man was a being still insufficiently prepared to acquire the likeness to God. On this account, since the Lemurian epoch, everything done by man was done less well than would otherwise have been the case. This applies above all to what regards himself. His astral, etheric and physical bodies, which but for the luciferic influence would have remained more spiritual, were, through that influence, less well formed, made more material. That was the reason of all the evil which developed in the life of man as time went on. In the course of a very long time have these evils developed.

From the Lemurian epoch to the Mystery of Golgotha they developed in the physical, etheric and astral bodies. In the astral body a high degree of egotism was developed ; in the etheric body the possibility of mistaken judg- ment and the possibility of lying. If man had remained under the influence of divine-spiritual beings, acting instinctively in accordance with their impulses, he would not to-day, when he desires knowledge of the world around him, be able to fall into error, nor could he be led into untruth. Thus did the tendency to lying and the danger of error find place in the development of man ; and since the spiritual is always the origin of the physical, and because the luciferic in- fluence and its consequences ate their way more and more deeply into the etheric body during incarnation after incarnation, the possibility of disease entered the physical body. Illness is the evil that entered the physical body through that development ; but something of still greater significance has come. If man had not been subject to these influences, if he had not allowed them to work upon him, he would never have supposed that anything more than a change of life takes place when the physical body falls away from us ; consciousness of death would not have come to him. If man had descended less deeply into matter

31

and had kept hold of the threads uniting him with the divine-spiritual, he would have been aware that when the physical sheath is laid aside, a new form of existence begins ; but he would never have looked upon that as a loss, as the end of an existence he had grown fond of. Everything in evolution would have taken on a different aspect.

Man descended more deeply into matter, he thus made himself more free and independent, but he also thereby made his own development more limited than it would have been.

Everything lacking in man will be made good by the Christ-Impulse ; but one must not expect that to be done in a short time nor even in a comparatively short time. A very long time elapsed between the Lemurian epoch and the Mystery of Golgotha. Slowly and gradually, during incarnation after incarnation, came egotism, error and lying, disease and the realisation of death. Man is being led back into the spiritual world, so to speak, with the qualities he has acquired " from below." The re-ascent will be a quicker progress than the descent ; but it cannot be expected that in one or two incarnations man will be enabled, through what he can take in of the Christ-Impulse, to overcome selfishness and to heal his etheric body to such an extent that all danger of lying and error is at an end, still less can he be expected to be able to work healingly on his physical body. All this must go on slowly and gradually ; but it is going on. Just as man has been led down into all those qualities by the luciferic impulse, so will he be led up out of them by the Christ-Impulse. Selfishness will be transmuted into selflessness, lying into truthfulness, the danger of error into absolute certainty and true judgment. Illness will become the foundation for more complete health ; the illness we have overcome will be the germs of greater good-health ; and when we have gradually learnt to understand death in such a way that the Death at Golgotha works as a prototype of death in our own soul, death will then have lost its sting. Man will then know why from time to time he must lay aside his physical covering, in order to rise higher and higher in the course of his embodiments. In particular, the Christ-Impulse brought with it the impulse to make good something connected with man's knowledge and observation, with his knowledge of the world.

We have said that man has become more entangled in matter, less perfect in his three bodies than he would have been if there had been no luciferic influence ; this caused him to be possessed by an urge to sink more deeply into material existence, to soak himself more completely in mere matter. This refers more especially to his knowledge, but even that only came about slowly and gradually. Man did not, as soon as the luciferic influence made itself felt, immediately sink down so deeply as to close all the doors into the spiritual world behind him. He still remained, for a long time, in connection with the spiritual world from which he grew forth and with which he would have remained in connection with his whole being, if the luciferic influence had not come. He long remained a participator in it ; for a long time he continued to feel that his finer, more spiritual instincts were guided by the threads from the divine-spiritual world. For a long time he still continued to feel that his impulse was not a merely human one, it was as though the Gods had been at work behind it. That was more particularly the case in more ancient times. Man was driven slowly into matter and he thus gradually lost the consciousness of the divine.

Those spiritual movements and world-conceptions of humanity which had knowledge of these things, have also hinted at this. They said : There was once upon a time an age in which man was driven some way into material existence by the luciferic influence—though not so far as to prevent the divine influence from still having a powerful effect upon him. In the early ages of man's development this was known as the 'Golden Age.' This is no fanciful conception : 'Golden Age' is simply the expression used by those men of olden times who still had an inkling that there had been something like a primeval age of humanity, such as has just been described. This Golden Age, known to Eastern philosophy as Krita-Yuga, lasted, comparatively speaking, much longer than the Ages we still have to describe. After the Golden Age came the so-called 'Silver Age.' Man was pushed further down into the physical world ; but the process went on slowly and gradually. Even then the doors of the spiritual world were not yet completely closed. Man still had intense moments in which, in a dreamy sort of clairvoyance, he saw the Gods at work behind his instincts. Man could no longer be called a companion of the Gods in this Silver Age, but he could still perceive them standing behind him. Eastern philosophy calls this age, Treta-Yuga. Then came an Age which extends into our own Post-Atlantean period ; its last stragglers extended into historical times when there still were people gifted with the old dream-like, twilight consciousness. The consciousness of a spiritual world from which man had come forth, still existed ; though only as a kind of memory remaining over from former incarnations. It was just as when we now remember our own childhood, our youth, and our present age. In childhood we had direct experience of our childish happenings ; in like manner man still experienced in Treta Yuga in a direct way, the impulse of a divine-spiritual world. In the Age following on that, known as the 'Bronze Age,' what man had was more like a memory. It might be compared with the way a grown man contemplates his childhood ; for we say : 'I experienced my childhood ; it was not a dream !' That was like the state of things in the Third Age. Men then knew : 'In earlier ages we had experience of communion with the Gods ; that is now nothing but a memory !' I have explained at some length how in the Old-Indian period of civilisation the memory of the Atlantean epoch worked retrospectively, thus enabling the holy Rishis to reveal their great divine teachings. This Bronze Age is known in Eastern philosophy as Dvapara-Yuga. That is followed by an Age in which all memory of the divine-spiritual world is lost, when man, with his knowledge and perception, is entirely given up to the physical world. That age began about the year 3101 B.C. In Eastern philosophy it is known as Kali-Yuga, 'the dark age' ; because man had then lost all connection with the spiritual world and become completely one with the physical world. I wish expressly to note that I am now using these expressions for smaller divisions of time, but they can also be applied to larger spans. We are now speaking of the divisions of time corresponding to the smaller ages, and we make Kali-Yuga begin, as does Indian philosophy, with the year 3101 before our era. The Age was then being prepared in which men were taught only to see that which conceals the divine-spiritual world as by a veil, by a covering; when they only perceived the external physical. At the beginning of Kali-Yuga there were still many who could either see or recollect the divine-spiritual world, but for normal humanity the time set in when they could only see the physical world of nature.

That was the descent of man to Kali-Yuga. It was the time of deepest descent. Into that had to come the impulse for re-ascent. That is why this impulse, the Christ-Impulse, had to come during the Kali-Yuga, in the ' dark ' age.

This Christ-Impulse was prepared for by the religion of Jahve or Jehovah; for this religion taught man how little reliance could be placed on his former decisions. During the time which extended from the old Lemurian epoch to the Revelation on Mount Sinai, we have that age in which man was given the power to choose good or evil, while at the same time he became liable to err in judging between them, and became more and more likely to bring on earth that which is known as ' Sin.' Sin then ate its way into the life of the earth. Man became ' like to the Gods,' but in return for this he acquired qualities which were in nowise ripe for the likeness to God. What had to happen then ? First of all man had to be shown what the Godhead expected from him if he was to become a self-conscious ego. This was shown to him by the announcement made on Mount Sinai in the ' Ten Commandments.' The people then heard proclaimed through Moses : ' The good and evil thou hast already developed are not sufficient. I will show thee how these Commandments should sound if thou hadst not descended, and in return for thy defective qualities, received the power of judging between good and evil.' The Decalogue, the law, given to man on Sinai, was given to man as he had then become ; so that out of the spiritual worlds man heard sounding forth that which was right, in contrast to what he had insufficiently developed. The Ten Commandments stand forth as a law of iron, as a torch, showing man what he had not become. He had to submit himself to that law, with all he had become. Man could not at first have submitted to the Ten Commandments, because he had become lacking in decision, lacking in self-guidance. Therefore, they had to be given to him by one who was inspired ,—by Moses—that is to say, they were given him from above by Divine administration. They were, however, given in such a way that they were intended for the ego. They told man how an ego must act, if it is to attain the goal of humanity.

In the lecture on ' *The Ten Commandments of Moses* ' (16th November, 1908) this is traced out in detail. Therein is first shown the right attitude of the ego to the spiritual worlds ; this is contained in the first three Commandments. The next ones refer to man's conduct towards his fellow-men in act and deed, and the last Commandments refer to the control of his feelings and sensations. The Ten Commandments give instructions for the education of the ego. This was the preparation by means of which the ego was to learn in its most inward being how to give itself the impulse after having descended into Kali-Yuga, into the age of darkness. At first man was to be given the Law from above. The Law of one's own ego could however, only become what it was to be, when that ego takes into itself the great Prototype of Golgotha, saying : ' If I take into my soul such thinking as was thought by the Being Who

34

offered Himself in sacrifice on Golgotha,—if I take into myself such feelings as were felt by the Being Who offered Himself as sacrifice on Golgotha,—if I take into myself such willing as was willed by the Being Who offered Himself in sacrifice on Golgotha, then will my being come to a decision within itself to develop increasingly a likeness to God, it will then no longer have to follow the Outer Law, the Ten Commandments, but an inner impulse, its own Law.'

Thus Moses first put before mankind the Law, but Christ gave them the Prototype and the strength which the soul ought to take in, whereby to develop itself. Hence all the spiritual impulses were to be taken into the innermost of the soul, even into the ego itself ; they were all to be deepened into inwardness through Christ Jesus. That could only take place if men thought as follows, and Christ Jesus radiated it forth as an impulse :—

Man has descended into the dark age, into Kali-Yuga. Before that dark age men saw into the spiritual world with a dim twilight consciousness. They were then able, not merely to make use of the instruments of the physical body, but when they observed the physical world through their eyes, ears and so on, they perceived the spiritual surrounding all things, flowers, plants, stones, etc. As regards this observation of the spiritual, men were rich in those days. In the older times the spirit was bestowed on them ; whereas, in the dark age, as regards the spirit they were reduced to beggary ; for the spirit was no longer bestowed upon them. They had become poor in spirit. Kali-Yuga came upon them more and more, that time when men had to say to themselves : In the old days things were different, the spirit was then bestowed on men ; they were able to look up into a spiritual world, they were then rich in spirit ; the kingdoms of heaven were then accessible to them. Now men are pressed down into the physical world. The gates of the spiritual world are closed to human senses, and no view of the kingdoms of heaven is open to the physical body. But Christ was able to say : ' Lay hold of the ego, where it must now be apprehended ! Then will the Kingdoms of Heaven draw near to you. They will arise within your own ego. Though the spiritual light may be concealed from your eyes behind the external light which is perceptible to the senses, though spiritual sound may be concealed from your ears behind physical sound ; yet, when Christ Himself shall raise you, ye shall find the Kingdoms of Heaven within you ! ' Unhappy were those who had become poor in the dark age, who had become beggars as regard the spirit. They can now become blessed, the impulse having been given through which Christ is able, from the spiritual world, from the Kingdoms of Heaven, to penetrate into the very ego or ' I ' of man. Therefore, with respect to man's poverty of spirit, the highest Christian proclamation is this : ' From henceforward, blessed are they who are beggars in spirit, who no longer receive the spirit bestowed upon them according to the old conception. Henceforth, they can be blessed if they take in the Christ-Impulse ; for, through the developing of their ego, the Kingdoms of Heaven will be within them.'

Let us pass on to the etheric body, which is the builder of the physical body. What has entered that ? Illness only expresses itself in the physical body. The trouble itself is first in the etheric body ; that then expresses itself in a subsequent incarnation as illness in the physical body. ' Now, however, something has entered the world,' so Christ Jesus had to say, 'whereby an impulse may arise within gradually to clear away the affliction from the etheric body. Blessed may those now be who have an affliction attached to their etheric bodies if they take up the Christ-Impulse; for they have something within them which lifts them above the suffering and teaches them to find inner comfort, the inner paraclete, the inner comforter!'

Now what had the astral body become through the luciferic influence? It had become less perfect than before. It had been given the possibility which we have described as a good quality: of being able to be aglow for what is great and good, to feel enthusiasm for the sublime treasures of the true, the beautiful and the good. On the other hand it has to purchase this at the price of feeling little or no sympathy or antipathy for the treasures of the earth. But a man who takes up the Christ-Impulse learns to control the astral body, which stirs his physical body to opposition to the treasures of the earth, he learns to bring it under the power of the spirit; and in so doing he becomes happy or blessed. 'Blessed will he be who makes his astral body indifferent to the things of earth; which will thereby fall to his share. For when he is all afire for the things of earth, feeling both emotion and sympathy or antipathy for them, he casts away that which they might become to him; but when the astral body is brought under the power of the spiritual and he grows indifferent to the things of earth, the Kingdom of Earth is added as a reward.'

Let us now ascend to that which works as sentient soul within the astral body. Herein we still possess in a dim sort of way, a ruling ego, an ego which has not yet wholly emerged and hence is still developing the most egotistical passions. As long as the ego is still really within the sentient soul, it develops the most selfish egoism. The wish that others should have the same as we have is lacking. Egoism dims the sense of justice, for the ego wants everything for itself. But if the ego transmutes itself in imitation of the Christ-Impulse, it will hunger and thirst after justice for all the beings around us. 'Blessed will be those who hunger and thirst after the feeling of justice in their sentient-soul; for they shall be satisfied.' They will be able to bring about conditions all over the world corresponding to the proper new spirit of justice in the depths of the soul.

Let us further ascend to the intellectual or mind soul. This principle brings about to a still greater extent the consideration of one man for another, not merely as a feeling of justice such as is produced by the sentient soul, but as compassion, a true compassion for the sorrows of others and a sharing in their joy. One who takes in the Christ-Impulse grows to feel what others feel, not only what he feels himself; he immerses himself in the ego of others and in so doing feels bliss in his intellectual or mind soul. Blessed is he who develops fellow-feeling; for only by feeling himself within the soul of others, does he stimulate them to feel themselves in him. He will receive the sympathy of others when he himself radiates fellow-feeling for them. 'Blessed are those who feel with others, for others shall feel with them.'

You will now see how, having gone a little further in our study of these connections, we are able to understand in a different way from the very depths of the nature and being of man, those words in St. Matthew's Gospel, generally

36

known as the Sermon on the Mount. Each sentence of the Sermon on the Mount relates to one of the nine principles of man. In the next lectures we will go further into this. The Sermon on the Mount must become transparent to our spiritual eyes as that deed of Christ Jesus by means of which he turned what was contained in the Old Law of Moses into something quite inward, an inner impulse enabling man's ego to become active, as it must become in all the nine principles of man. For if the ego takes up the Christ-Impulse it affects all these.

Thus we see the profound truth of what I already indicated here once before : that in Kali-Yuga Christ made the ego of man capable of discovering something in the physical world which can lead man up into the spiritual world, into the Kingdoms of Heaven. Christ has made the ego of man a participator in the spiritual world. On ancient Saturn the physical body was taken straight out of the spiritual world. It was still within that world, because the physical body was at that time much more spiritual and was not aware that it could separate from the spiritual worlds. The etheric body was added on the Sun and the astral body on the Moon, but only on the earth was it made possible—through the development of the ego—to set oneself free from the divine-spiritual. In consequence of this, as the ego must be led back again, God had to descend to the physical plane, and on that plane show man how to find the way back to the Kingdoms of Heaven.

A most important event was brought about through the Christ-Impulse. Now just ask yourselves this question : Did all those living at the time when Christ Jesus worked on earth know that such an important event was taking place ? Just reflect that Tacitus—the great historian, mentions the Christians as an almost unknown sect. A hundred years after Christ he only mentions the Christians as a sect living in a side-street in Rome, whose teacher was a certain Jesus ; they are simply mentioned as living there. For a long time after the Christ-Event many people in Rome believed Jesus was a contemporary of theirs, as though he had only just appeared. In short, important events can take place in the evolution of man, without contemporaries noticing that anything has happened. The most important things may come about and pass unobserved if people do not cultivate the understanding for them. They would then miss the experience, and as far as that was concerned they would be barren and dried up. 'Change your hearts ! The Kingdoms of Heaven have approached !' That was the proclamation of John the Baptist and of Christ Jesus Himself. They hinted to those who had ears to hear that something most important was occurring. That nothing is known in the world of an important happening is no proof that it is not taking place. Those whose business it is to-day to point out the signs of the times, are aware of what is taking place to-day. They must point to an occurrence which, though not one of the most cogent, is yet important. True it is that just in our own time something of infinite significance is developing. Just as John pointed to Christ, and Christ Himself pointed to the approach of the Kingdoms of Heaven, to the ego ; so must we to-day point to another important event.

Christ descended once to the earth in a body of flesh ; He spent the first years of our era on earth, in the flesh. In accordance with the wise guidance of our world-evolution it is not ordained that men should again see Christ in the flesh, as a physically incarnated man ; nor is it necessary that they should. For Christ will not return in the flesh. Why ? Because what we call the dark age—the Kali-Yuga—was completed at the end of the ninteenth century, and because with the twentieth century began a new age, in which men must prepare to develop new capacities, those faculties which were lost in the dark age. Slowly and gradually these are being prepared. These faculties will develop so far that single individuals will be here who will possess them as natural tendencies. These faculties will be seen in a certain number of persons, particularly between the years of 1930 and 1940, and by means of these a number of people will enter into new relation with the Christ.

This indicates an important point in human development. Spiritual Science is here to open the understanding of men to these new faculties which will be developed in the world of men. Anthroposophy has not come into the world because a few people are in sympathy with it and would like to make it further known ; it has come because it is wanted if people wish to understand what will take place in the first half of this century. For it is only by means of that which Spiritual Science can give mankind that it will become capable of understanding this. When people become capable of perceiving in the spirit that which will then occur, they will also be incapable of confusing that event with their mistaken representations. For as materialism spreads further, it will extend even to the spiritual conception of the world where it will have a particularly evil influence. In that realm it might tend to prevent men from understanding what should be spiritually comprehended. What should really be grasped in the spirit they will seek in the world of matter. Because we are to enter into a new relation to Christ in the course of the first half of our century, it must over and over again be emphasised during the next decades and until the event occurs, that false Messiahs, false Christs will arise who will knock at the doors of those who are only able to be materialists in the realms of Spiritual Science, and can only imagine a new relation to Christ if they see Him before them in the flesh. A number of false Messiahs will turn this to their own use, saying : ' Christ has reappeared in the flesh ! '

Anthroposophical wisdom has the duty of preparing the relation which can be attained during the first half of our century by purely human capacities. The responsibility of the Anthroposophical effort becomes ever greater and greater, for it has to prepare for a coming event which will only be understood if Anthroposophy makes its way into the souls of men and thus becomes fruitful for the further development of humanity. The alternative is that men will neglect to accept and make use of the instrument of Spiritual Science, through which this Event can be understood ; in that case it will pass humanity by uncomprehended. For if men so entirely reject Spiritual Science that nothing of it should remain, they would not know that this event is there or would interpret it wrongly. The fruit of this event would then be lost to the future of humanity, and man would thus be thrust down into dreadful misery.

I have thus hinted at a new relation to the Christ which is germinating in the souls of men and which they will be able to evolve in a comparatively near future.

LECTURE 4.

THE SERMON ON THE MOUNT.

Berlin, 8th February, 1910.

To-day we must again refer to the old and important teaching contained in the Beatitudes of the Sermon on the Mount, and, starting from that we shall carry forward our vision to our own times and the near future.

The Sermon on the Mount as reported in St. Matthew's Gospel can only be understood if we grasp the whole spirit of it, in the sense of the development of all humanity. Let us briefly recapitulate what was put before us in the last lecture : that the old dim clairvoyance of man had gradually receded and that the capacities and knowledge of man had to be more and more limited to the physical plane, and that for this reason the connection of man with the Spiritual worlds had to be based on an event on the physical plane. If we recollect all this we shall understand that the Divine-Spiritual Being whom we have characterised as the Christ, had to embody Himself in a physical body at the very time when the perception of man had become limited to the physical plane. This was done so that the most essential part of the life of this Divine-Spiritual Being could be described in words and expressions used on the physical plane. The important point is not so much that few persons (in comparison to the whole of humanity) were able to have a bodily perception and observation of Christ Jesus, as that what is related of Him is a presentation of events on the physical plane. For it cannot be said that the earlier records of other Divinities related in words belonging to the physical plane refer to actual physical events. In everything that we are told of these, words can only be useful as indications ; —for what occurred with respect to these Divinities can only be understood by one able to apply the words to the events of higher planes. The life of Christ Jesus can however, be understood by anyone who can apply what is told to the events of the physical plane. In reference to this we can say : The Christ-Being descended into a physical embodiment, into complete life in a physical body. That had to be because human capacities at that time were of this nature, and because the human ego as such had to become conscious of its being if evolution was to go forward in the right way.

We have seen that the most important of the older intermediaries for the event of Golgotha was Zarathustra or Zoroaster. In order that he might become what he was to be, at that time a body had to be prepared, containing an extract, as it were, of what had been given to a whole people, a people who had to give to humanity the qualities which can only be communicated through physical inheritance. We have seen that the most essential thing in the old

39

Hebrew people was the duty of developing in successive generations, from father to son, from son to grandson, and so on, those qualities which had to be inherited in a continually increased form, till they finally appear in their highest and best form in the body which was derived by inheritance from Abraham and Solomon and which was finally occupied by Zarathustra. We have a great deal more to learn through our studies before we shall be able to understand the full mission of the old Hebrew people, in all its details. This necessitates that we should gradually learn how the qualities needed for the body of Jesus were more and more ennobled in the course of the descent from generation to generation. It had to be made as perfect as possible for the fulfilment of its world-historical mission, for that mission could only be carried out if all that pertained to the body of the Solomonian Jesus Being was as perfect as possible in itself as regards those qualities. Now we know that the four principles of man's nature, the physical body, etheric body, astral body and ego, are active in every human body; and that in time to come Spirit-self, Life-Spirit and Spirit-man, will also be active therein. This must not be taken to mean that the activity of the astral body will suddenly cease, or that the later is not being prepared in the earlier. In a certain respect everything that follows later must be prepared in what went before. Of course man cannot of his own strength so work upon himself to-day that the Life-Spirit, for instance, could come to particular expression within him; but in him work other Divine Spiritual Beings, with an activity which may be called an activity of the Life Spirit. This applies also to Spirit-man. Therefore, all the seven principles of the body, or rather of the human organism of Jesus of Nazareth had to be ennobled, as regards the qualities which had to be dealt with. This required very special preparation. This preparation may to-day give us an inkling of the secrets concealed in the development of humanity and of the earth.

The germs of the perfection in the body of Jesus of Nazareth had to be prepared long before. We have seen how during the first period (extending from Abraham to Solomon or David), the generations were worked upon just as a man's physical body is worked upon during the time between his birth and the change of teeth. This work was so performed by the forces active behind evolution, that at a certain time there was actually an ancestor of Jesus who already contained within him, capacities as nearly perfect as possible, and these re-appeared in the body which became the vehicle of Zarathustra. Thus in an ancestor of Jesus the foundations of a right development of all the seven principles of man's nature were present. In other words: If we trace back the ancestry of Jesus, we must find one ancestor who possessed the germ of the seven-principled-nature—although not so perfectly developed as in the body of Jesus of Nazareth—yet present in rudimentary form. Although not expressed in their external tradition, the secret doctrine of the ancient Hebrews was cognisant of this fact. It was aware that once upon a time a man lived of whom it must be said that the seven principles worked in him in such a way that they had to be described as quite peculiarly worthy of note! The Initiates of the old Hebrew secret doctrine actually pointed to an ancestor of Jesus of Nazareth, knowing that he possessed these seven human principles in a quite remarkable degree!

They called the ego of this ancestor, 'Itiel,' to indicate that in him the ego must have possessed that force (for Itiel signifies something like 'possessor of force'). He must have possessed that dauntlessness, which would, when carried down through the generations, become the proper ego-vehicle for the high being who was to reappear in Jesus of Nazareth. In the same way they called the astral body of this ancestor 'Lemuel'; that would more or less describe an astral body so far developed that it does not merely feel the law, the conformity to law, outside itself, but feels that it bears the law within it. They called the etheric body of this ancestor 'Ben Jage'; that would signify an etheric body as far as possible transmuted within, which having attained a certain perfection, is able to take habits into itself. The physical body of this ancestor they called 'Agur', because the physical activity, the capacity of this ancestor on the physical plane, consisted in his having assimilated everything brought over from old tradition; for 'Agur' signified 'a collector.' All the ancient conceptions of the world, all the old traditions, were gathered together in Jesus; and the rudiments of this were already developed in this ancestor. What worked as Spirit-Man in this ancestor, was called, (because the Divine-Spiritual Beings gave loving attention to their work on the rudiments of Spirit-Man,) 'Jedidjah', a word signifying something like 'the darling of the Gods'. What worked in this ancestor as Buddhi or Life-Spirit, was called 'Kohelet'; for it was said: 'In this ancestor there must have worked a Life-Spirit which was able to act as a teacher to the whole nation, so that its content could be poured out to them all'. And finally, Manas or Spirit-self in this ancestor was known by the word, 'Salomo', which signifies inner balance, for they said: Such a Spirit-self must have had within it the rudiments of being inwardly whole, of being in a state of balance within. Thus this ancestor, who is usually known only by the name of Schelomo, Schleimo, or Solomon, has three principal names: Jedidjah, Kohelet, Salomo; and four additional names: Agur, Ben Jage, Lemuel and Itiel, for these names signify the four coverings, whereas the three first names signify the divine inner part. The secret doctrine of the old Hebrews had seven names for this person. If later, people were dissatisfied with Solomon, as was the case even among certain sects of the Jews themselves. (whether rightly or wrongly cannot be gone into here), this can easily be accounted for. In Solomon there were great, important rudiments, which were to be further propagated for a distinct purpose. Now an individual human being, at a definite stage of his evolution, does not always display in his outer life the germs of the qualities he is to bequeath to his descendants; perhaps for the very reason that such great forces are within him he may even be more subject to failure in this direction. The lack of morality to be observed in Solomon is not in contradiction to what the old Hebrew secret doctrine saw in him; on the contrary it would explain his failings.

Thus the old Jewish secret doctrine looks back to an ancestor of Jesus, fully conscious of his significance for the whole mission of their people. All that was but rudimentary in this personality, was propagated by descent through the generations, and appeared in its essence when it was required and made use of in the course of the world's history. This may give us an inkling of the secrets, regulated by laws, which lie behind the evolution of mankind.

Now if the mission of the old Hebrew people pre-eminently consisted in the fact that through the physical inheritance certain capacities are, as it were, instilled into their blood capacities to be given to all mankind from the Spiritual world through this people, then, at the time of the appearance of John the Baptist and Jesus of Nazareth, humanity ought to have been sufficiently advanced to be able, through these ennobled capacities, to reascend into the Spiritual world; in other words it ought to have been able to take up the Christ-Impulse. I have told you all this to show what preparations were necessary in order, in the development of physical humanity, to create a sheath capable of enclosing the Christ-Being.

We can now perhaps feel and realise the intrinsic nature of the progress in the mission of humanity brought about by the descent of the Divine mission into physical matter, in the Jewish people. We can feel how the Divine was carried down into the depths of physical matter, in order that from this turning-point man might reascend so much the higher, from the now finer physical into the Spiritual. The ascent into the Spiritual had to begin from that time. For this however, an impulse had to be given to mankind which should to some degree place all that man can desire or expect from evolution into that deepest centre in man's being which can be designated as the ego. Through Christ, the impulse was to penetrate to the depths of man's inner being, out of the body of Christ there spoke such an impulse as called to the deepest part of man's nature. What was to be made different by this impulse?

Before this impulse came, all that brought happiness to men, that gave them bliss and made them feel ' filled with the Divine,' came to them in a sense from without; they expected it to come thence. If we do not merely study the history of the world from external documents but according to what the Spiritual records can give us, we must say that we look back to ancient times, when man ascended to the realm of Spiritual beings through arousing in himself,—whether by normal means or not,—the gift of clairvoyance. But this vision awoke in a dreamy way; Divine-Spiritual forces worked in it and the ego was suppressed. Man was more or less outside his ego. Although in his normal state he was not so conscious of his ego as he became later, yet he was then in the age when the spirit worked within him and carried him outside himself, without his ego into the Spiritual world. He yielded himself completely, either to the external Divine-Spiritual or to the Divine-Spiritual within his soul. But during that time of ecstasy, of enchantment, he was not in any sense conscious of his condition. The time was still to come when man would realise the relation to the spirit in his own ego, and thence permeate the deepest core of his being with the consciousness: I belong to a Divine-Spiritual kingdom. That could only come about through Christ pouring His own Being into the earth-being, so that the ego could permeate itself with what was the pattern of Christ. That enabled man to say: ' I am now in a Spiritual realm, in the Kingdoms of Heaven with my ego,' whereas man formerly entered the Kingdoms of Heaven while outside it. ' The Kingdom of Heaven has drawn near,' was the teaching given. For this the minds of men had to be changed, they were no longer to believe that they could only enter the Spiritual world in a state of ecstasy, for they would be able to find their relation to the Kingdoms of Heaven in full ego-consciousness.

We can see that this had to take place, for the old clairvoyant condition had, in the course of thousands of years, grown worse and worse. Whereas in olden times man, when in ecstasy ascended to the good Divine-Spiritual powers, that which still remained of the old ecstatic condition at the time of the founding of Christianity, had become such that when man was now outside himself he did not ascend to the good but to the evil spiritual powers. That is the great difference between the two states of development. In ancient times when man dreamily rose into the Spiritual worlds by the suppression of his ego—'mediumistically' as we should say to-day—he was then in the company of the good Spiritual beings. This had become different at the time when man was to find the way into the Kingdom of Heaven with his ego; when he now sought or brought about the states of ecstasy, they are described as being states of 'obsession,' which brought him into connection with evil hostile spiritual powers. So at the time of the appearance of Christ Jesus the following had to be proclaimed as a healing doctrine: 'It is not right for you to try without your ego to get into a condition in which you can become aware of the Spiritual worlds; the right way now is to seek contact with the Divine-Spiritual worlds in the deepest core of your being!'

This is essentially the teaching contained in the Sermon on the Mount of St. Matthew's Gospel. We might re-write it thus: In olden times there was a dream-like clairvoyance. In this man was, in ecstasy, transported into the Spiritual worlds. At that time he was rich in Spiritual life; he was no beggar in the spirit as he became when Christianity was founded. When in olden times he was filled with the spirit, with what the Greeks called 'Pneuma', he was transported into the Spiritual worlds. Christ could not now say: 'Blessed or God-filled are those who in their ecstatic states become rich in the spirit, for these are the very ones who will certainly be healed'! He now had to proclaim: 'The time has come when blessed or God-filled are those who have become beggars in the spirit!' That means, those who can no longer rise into ecstatic dreamy clairvoyant conditions, but who are obliged to seek the Kingdom of Heaven within, from out of their ego.

Formerly, when man was placed amidst the sorrows and sufferings of earth, he only had to call forth within him the state in which he could be transported into the Divine-Spiritual worlds. He was not obliged to endure suffering, for when it came to him, he could at once seek the state in which he was filled with the spirit, God-filled, and in that state—severed from his ego—he could find balm for the sorrows and sufferings of earth. Christ Jesus had to proclaim that this time too was now past and over. Those would now be blessed, or God-filled, who, while they could no longer look outside for help for their sufferings, might through the strengthening of their own ego seek within themselves the power to find the Paraclete in their inner being. 'Blessed (God-filled) are they who do not banish sorrow by ecstatically raising themselves to the Divinity, but who endure it, developing the power of the ego whereby they can find within themselves the Paraclete, known later as the Holy Ghost who reveals himself through the Ego.' Even Buddha in his time did not recommend that sorrow should be endured, but that it should be thrown off, with all the thirst of earth. Even six hundred years before Christ Jesus, Buddha described sorrow and suffering on earth as the worst consequences of the longing for existence. Six hundred years later, in the Sermon on the Mount, Christ in the second Beatitude proclaimed that sorrow must not be done away with in that way, but must be endured, that it was a trial through which the Ego might develop the strength it can find within itself : the inner support of the Paraclete. This is literally contained in the second sentence of the Sermon on the Mount, even to the expression : Paraclete. It is only necessary to read these things in the right way. That is precisely the task of our age ; we must learn, through what is given to us in Spiritual Science, to read the great scriptures of old aright, through the teachings of Spiritual Science.

A third point is this. In olden times, when men could permeate themselves with what came to them in ecstasy and which the Greeks called ' Pneuma' or Spirit, they were then guided instinctively in their course. All their impulses, actions, emotions and desires—in fact, all that dwells in the astral body of man —was instinctively guided, when man was able to raise himself to the good Spiritual beings. He had not yet tried from his own ego to control and purify his inner passions and desires and to bring them into balance. Now, however, the time had come—and Christ was to proclaim this—when men having tamed, purified and balanced the passions, desires and impulses of this astral body— would of themselves reach the goal for the humanity of to-day, to which we give expression by pointing to the great progress of evolution. This has often been presented to us in the following way. Man began his existence on ancient Saturn ; he continued it through the Sun and Moon-existence, until on the earth the ego was added to him. Only when he becomes conscious of this ego, when he tames and balances what was added to him by the astral body on the Moon, can he really attain to the goal of the earth-mission. Those who are able to control and balance the desires in their astral body can be blessed (God-filled), for by this means they will, through themselves, discover the Earth. Thus the third sentence of the Sermon on the Mount, which as usually translated contains a meaningless word, tells us the following : Those who ' balance ' their passions desires and emotions (not make them ' meek ') to them shall be given—or they shall ' inherit '—the earth.

Thus the three first sentences of the Sermon on the Mount in their world-wide significance, place before us the following summary.

The first sentence of the Sermon on the Mount refers to the physical body, and informs us that it was formerly possible, in the olden times of humanity through a particular training of the physical body to perceive the Spiritual in clairvoyant dreamy conditions, but the physical body has now become poor as regards the inner possession of the spirit.

As regards the etheric body, through which man becomes conscious of suffering—although he is first aware of it in the astral body—the indication is given that men must learn to develop in themselves a force which will enable them to find help for the suffering which is given them as a trial.

Thirdly, we come on to the astral body, concerning which we are told, that through the taming and purifying of his impulses and passions man will find in his inner being the strength which will enable him to become a real ego, one to whom the earth mission is then allotted as his portion.

When we now ascend to the Ego, we know that this works in the sentient soul, intellectual soul and spiritual soul. The ego works in the sentient soul, that is : it spiritualises it. This enables man to feel the outpouring of human brotherly love—which becomes universal through the spreading of Christianity —as righteousness: ' hunger and thirst after the all-ruling righteousness '. The sentient soul otherwise feels only in the physical body ; it must now, through Christianity, learn to feel for spiritual things : to hunger and thirst after righteousness. Those who are able to find their human centre in the ego, will, as a result of their work on themselves, satisfy the longing in their sentient soul for an all-ruling earthly righteousness. ' Blessed are they who, through the Christ-Impulse, learn to hunger and thirst after righteousness ; for they will find a strong force in their inner being whereby, because they are working for the righteousness of the world, they shall find within themselves the satisfaction of this quality.'

We now come to the intellectual soul. We have often emphasised the fact that whereas in the sentient soul the ego is as yet but dimly brooding, in the intellectual soul it begins to shine forth, later to attain full consciousness in the spiritual soul where it first becomes a pure ego. In the intellectual soul something very singular happens : the human ego—*i.e.*, that wherein we each resemble all other men, for each of us bears the ego within him—shines forth. No matter in what part of the world we meet with our fellow-man, through the fact that an ego shines out of his intellectual soul he is a human being like ourselves. Something shines forth from our intellectual soul, and if we receive it as well as we can and carry it out into the world, we can enter into the right relation with our fellow-men. In our intellectual soul we are to develop something which we must pour forth into our surroundings and which must flow back to us again. That is why this is the only occasion in the Sermon on the Mount when the subject of the Beatitude is like the predicate, ' Blessed (or God-filled) are they who develop love ; for as they radiate forth love, it will return to them again.' This shows the infinite depths of such a spiritual document, for it can be understood by the very way in which the sentences are constructed, it can be understood even down to the smallest details, if gradually, year after year, one collects all that Spiritual Science can give for the understanding of man. The difference between the fifth Beatitude and the others, in all of which the subject and the predicate are different, cannot in the least be understood without knowing that the fifth Beatitude points directly to the intellectual soul, or Mind-soul. We will now ascend to the work of the ego on the Spiritual or Consciousness soul. Here at last the ego is pure and unalloyed ; only here can it become conscious of itself. This is beautifully expressed in the Sermon on the Mount, in the verse which expresses that only in the ego can the divine substance in man come to life. ' Blessed are they, who are pure in blood or in heart (which is the expression of the ego),who allow nothing to enter there but the pure ego-nature ; for they will recognise God therein, they will perceive God ! '

The Sermon on the Mount now rises to that which refers to the Spirit-Self,

Life-Spirit, and Spirit-Man. Here man can no longer work through himself alone ; at this stage of his evolution he must appeal to the divine Spiritual worlds, which, through Christ, have been brought into connection with the earth ; he must look up to the renewed divine spiritual worlds. Whereas in former times strife and disharmony entered humanity through the ego-nature— as indeed it still does to-day—peace will be poured out over the earth through the Christ-Impulse. And those who take up the Christ-Impulse will become the founders of peace in that part of human nature which in the future will gradually develop as Spirit-Self ; they will thus in a new sense become the sons of God, in that they will bring down the spirit from the Spiritual Realms—' Blessed are they who bring peace—or harmony into the world ; for they shall thereby be the sons of God ! ' Thus must they be called, who are really filled inwardly with a spirit self which is to bring peace and harmony on the earth.

Now, we must clearly understand, that of all that develops on the earth, some part survives into later ages. This, in a certain respect, is hostile to what implants itself as a germ in later ages. What the Christ-Impulse brings, enters into the whole evolution of humanity—it does not, however, enter all at once, but rather in such a way that something still remains from the earlier stages of evolution. It is therefore necessary that those who first understand this Christ-Impulse should stand firm on the basis thereof, quite permeated inwardly with its force. If they are inwardly permeated by the force that proceeds from the seed that has come from the Christ and stand firm on that foundation, they will then be blessed in a new sense ; in this they develop the force of firmness. ' Blessed are they who stand under the new order, who stand under Christ and who suffer persecution from that which remains over from the old order ! ' And the last of the beatitudes of the Sermon on the Mount points straight to the Christ-Impulse itself, for He says to the Apostles : Blessed are ye, who are especially called to carry the Name of Christ out into the world ! '

Thus we see how the Sermon on the Mount directs Christianity from out of the great teachings of cosmology and humanity, while everywhere directing attention to the force within, the centre point of which must be found in the Ego itself. The time has now come when this must be understood, and understood in such a way that people must not believe themselves to be true Christians because they try to find Christianity in some dogmatic collateral signification or side issue, but rather those are true Christians who understand the meaning of the text : ' Change the disposition of your souls, for the kingdoms of heaven have descended even into the ego ! ' Those persons can be called ' Christians ' in the true sense who realise that this is the essential point, and who further understand that this had to be put at the beginning of our era in a different way from that in which it must be given out now ! It would be a mistaken idea of Christianity to believe that what was considered Christian in the words spoken two thousand years ago has not since then undergone further development. Christianity would stand for nothing but a dead stream of culture. But it is a living one ! It is developing, and will continue to develop ! Just as it is true that Christianity had to start from the time when man had descended right down to the physical plane, when a Divine Being became man in a physical human body, so it is also true that at our present time man must learn to rouse himself to the understanding of Christianity and of the Christ Being Itself, from a Higher Spiritual Standpoint !—What does this mean ?

Just as it is true that the old dreamy clairvoyant forces had been lost, so that at the time of Christ those persons who were filled 'with God' in the old sense could no longer be described as 'blessed,' but only such as formed the kingdoms of Heaven within them, it is also true that the ego of man will re-ascend into the Spiritual world in full consciousness and will develop ever new forces and capacities. Just as it is true that the time of the Baptist was the time when those capacities which led down to the physical plane had reached a crisis in humanity, it is also true that we have now again reached an important time. What is called the 'Dark Age,' which began in the year 3101 B.C. and reached its height at the time of the Incarnation, came to an end at the close of the 19th Century. The Kali-Yuga was concluded in 1899 ! We are now approaching a time when new forces and capacities will be developed by man and these will be distinctly apparent in the last half of our present century. These new forces and capacities must be understood. Particularly those persons who have studied and understood Anthrosophy must realise that such an uplifting of humanity towards the Spiritual has again become possible. For during the important times that will follow after 1930, single individuals will find it possible to develop higher forces in their nature, whereby what we know as the etheric body will become visible. A certain number of people will develop etheric clairvoyant powers.

One of two things will then be possible, either the materialism of our age will continue, in which case when these forces are manifested men will fail to understand that they lead into the Spiritual worlds ; they will then be wrongly understood and so be crushed. Should that occur, would not people, speaking in a materialistic sense at the end of the year 1940, be justified in saying: 'Now see what fantastic prophets those were who spoke at the beginning of the 20th century ! Nothing of what they foretold has been fulfilled.' But if the new capacities have not appeared, that would not contradict what may be said now, and must indeed be said ; it would only prove that people without the right understanding have choked them in the bud and that they have missed something which humanity must possess if its further evolution is not to collapse into dissolution and decay. That is the great responsibility of Anthroposophy. Anthroposophy has sprung from a knowledge of the necessity for an advanced preparation for something which will come, but which might be overlooked and suppressed. Anthroposophy has the task of bringing about an understanding of the Spiritual forces developing in man. If these forces are suppressed humanity will sink deeper into the mire of materialism.

On the other hand, Anthroposophy may be successful in spreading through its teachings an understanding of the fact that man must rise into the Spiritual worlds ; it may succeed in lifting mankind out of the materialistic frame of mind. For this, however, something must now come forth from the anthroposophical movement, something that was prepared centuries ago, but which must now, in our own age, evolve to a particular and important turning-point.

47

The centuries that lie behind us were fitted for cultivating to an increasing extent the materialistic ideas of man. Under this materialistic influence it was easy to believe that the Christ-Impulse and the Christ-Being would come into touch with the world by incarnating once again—or perhaps oftener—in a physical, material body. Instead of acquiring clear notions of the fact that men must grow up as regards their capacities so that a great number, and finally all, might experience the Event of Damascus—that is : might experience the Christ in the atmosphere around the earth, and see Him in His etheric body—it was believed that Christ would descend again in a physical body, for the materialistic satisfaction of those who refuse to believe in the spirit, and who will not believe what St. Paul saw in the Event of Damascus : that Christ is in the Earth-atmosphere and that He is always there ! ' I am with you always, even unto the end of the world ! ' Those who develop the methods of clairvoyant vision into the Spiritual world will find what could not be found there in the pre-Christian time : the Christ in His etheric body. That is the important progress in the evolution of humanity ; before the first half of our century has elapsed, those faculties by means of which the event of Damascus becomes a personal experience, will develop naturally as it were, and men will see the Christ in His etheric body. He will not descend into flesh, but man will ascend when he has acquired understanding of the spirit.

That is the manner of Christ's return in our own age, for in this 20th century men must work their way up out of the Kali-Yuga into a century of clairvoyance. They must ascend to Christ by means of the capacities which they will develop ; they must ascend to the Christ where He is and where He can be seen, at first sight, by those in the vanguard, those who through the teachings of Anthroposophy can be guided to what in the course of the next 2,500 years will be experienced to a greater or less degree by every human soul.

The great event which awaits mankind in the near future is, that those who raise themselves—with full Ego-consciousness—to the etheric vision of Christ in His etheric body, will be ' God-filled ' or blessed. For this, however, the materialistic mind must be thoroughly overcome, and men must acquire understanding of Spiritual doctrine and Spiritual life.

In bygone centuries it was, comparatively speaking, not harmful for men continually to return to the materialistic conception of the so-called return of Christ. Particularly at the small times of transition, when that which has now reached its climax in a materialistic sense was being prepared for, as, for instance, in France in 1137, when a Messiah was expected, and was awaited by many in wide circles. A Messiah did actually appear then, but he led the people astray, because the belief in him had arisen through their materialistic ideas, for it was believed the Messiah would come in the flesh. Thirty years before, another Messiah appeared in Spain ; there, too, it had been foretold that a Messiah would come in the flesh. At about the same time another new Messiah appeared in North Africa ; there, too, it had been prophesied that one would come from the East, and appear in the flesh. Throughout the whole time during which the materialistic mind was being prepared, in that the highest things were being grasped by it, there appeared such prophets whose coming was foretold. Such phenomena are well known to those who understand the times, and they continued into the 17th century, when the approaching appearance of a sort of Christ, a Messiah, was proclaimed far and wide. This again found acceptance by the materialistically religious minds of men. Based on these prophecies, a false Messiah was thus able to arise in Smyrna, in 1667, bearing the name of Shabbathoi Zewi. He wrote letters and epistles at that time from Smyrna, which, although they contained nothing but false matter, being written in a materialistic sense, shook the world as greatly as had once the Epistles of St. Paul. In the 17th century there went forth from Smyrna the proclamation that in that city there dwelt a Messiah in the flesh! And Shabbathoi Zewi, the 'just man of God' was so considered, that it was said the whole world-reckoning would now take on another form. 'He will pass through the world with his faithful disciples and all must believe in him who are willing to see the truth, who wish to see Christ in the flesh!' It was preached to the people that his birthday must be held as the greatest Festival on Earth! Whole hosts of people undertook pilgrimages there—not only from Asia and Africa, but also from Poland, Russia, Spain, France, and so on; great numbers of persons travelled as pilgrims to Smyrna to see Shabbathoi Zewi, who was supposed to be Christ in the flesh, until the thing grew beyond all limits and he was arrested by order of the Sultan! This, said the people, was but the fulfilment of the prophesy, for it was foretold he would be in prison for nine months! The Sultan could think of no other method than to have him brought forth and stripped, saying: 'We will see whether thou be a Messiah, a Christ; I shall have thee shot!' And so it was finally proved that Shabbathoi Zewi was only an ordinary Ba Rabbi after all!

Such impersonations are the result of the materialistic thinking of our times, and there will be more of the kind, for the materialistic mind will make use of men.

What I am now saying will often and often be said during the next few decades: that the capacities of man will develop up to seeing the Etheric vision of Christ, in the reality of which they can then believe, just as firmly as did St. Paul himself! This is the immediate future of man, and this it is for which Spiritual Science must prepare him. But on account of the materialistic thoughts of men the time will also come when strong temptations will arise; false Messiahs will appear in the flesh. It will then be proved whether Anthroposophists have rightly understood Anthroposophy. Those who have not will be so adversely affected by the materialistic mind that they will succumb to the temptation. Although they believe in Christ they will believe in an incarnated Christ. But those who have gained understanding of true Spiritual life will realise that the 'second Coming of Christ' in our century, that greatest of Events, signifies that He comes to man in the Spirit, because mankind in the course of its development will have developed up to the Spiritual, will have evolved up towards Christ! Therefore in our century, the Sermon on the Mount undergoes a complete modification. It must be entirely re-modelled, so to speak. Those persons will be God-filled (or blessed) who, through having been beggars for the spirit in their past incarnations, have now advanced so far as to be able to ascend to that part of the kingdom of Heaven where Christ will appear before their spiritual sight!

Every single sentence of the Sermon on the Mount in its present form might be reconstructed in this sense. Christianity will only re-conquer its ancient documents when they are grasped in a living sense, when it is realised that they are living, not dead writings. When the time comes—and that time is here now—when materialistical research extends to the Gospel and takes away the tradition of Christ, then, as we have often stated, Spiritual research will give back the Gospels to mankind ! This coincidence will not be accidental, it will come of necessity. It may be that in our own time—during which the materialistic mind having gone as far as it can, will reach a crisis—certain unfortunate persons having, through their mistaken philosophy been led into curious ideas, may conclude that effects may be produced without causes, and that there never was an historical Jesus-Christ. This should be comprehensible to Anthroposophists. They ought, indeed, to feel a certain pity for those poor men who, notwithstanding their philosophy, are so entangled in materialistic thought that they have altogether lost the faculty of imagining the existence of spirit, and who, consequently, keep flying in the face of the saying, that there is no effect without a cause. Christianity as an effect could not have existed without a cause ! Anthroposophy, speaking from spiritual investigation, will tell men of Christ in the form in which He now lives, if they will but listen with an understanding mind. The understanding must be sufficiently matured to recognise definitely that the Christ will reappear, but as a reality higher than a physical one, a reality to which one can only look up, after first having acquired a sense and an understanding for spiritual life.

Inscribe in your hearts that Anthroposophy must be a preparation for the great epoch of humanity which is immediately ahead of us. Do not in this look upon it as matter of the first importance whether the souls now incarnated are still incarnated in physical bodies when Christ appears in the manner described, or whether they will then have already passed through the Portal and stand in the life between death and rebirth. For that which takes place in the 20th century is not of importance to the physical world alone, but to all the worlds with which man is connected. Just as those persons who will be in incarnation between 1930 and 1950 will experience the vision of the Etheric Christ, so a mighty revolution will also take place in the world in which man lives between death and rebirth. Just as Christ after the Mystery of Golgotha descended into the underworld, so will the effects of the Event which will occur for the inhabitants of the physical plane, rise into the spiritual plane. Those people who have not been prepared for this by Spiritual Science will miss the great and mighty Event, which will also take place in the Spiritual worlds in which man then lives. Those persons will have to wait for a new incarnation to experience on earth what makes them capable of receiving the new Christ-Impulse. For it is on earth that we must acquire the capacity of grasping all the Christ-Impulses, no matter how high they may lead us ! Not in vain has man been placed in the physical world ; for it is here we must acquire that which leads us to an understanding of the Christ-Impulse ! For all the souls now living, Anthroposophy is the preparation for the Christ-Event that awaits us in the near future. This preparation is necessary. Other events will follow this Christ Event in the course of the development of mankind. It will therefore be a great omission, if those who have the opportunity of raising themselves during this century to the Christ-Event, do not take advantage of it.

Only if we look upon Anthroposophy in this way and inscribe it in our souls, can we realise what it means to each human soul and what it ought to become to all humanity.

———

LECTURE 5.

CORRESPONDENCES BETWEEN THE MICROCOSM AND THE MACROCOSM.

Berlin, 9th March, 1910.

Our lecture to-day will consist of a kind of summing up of all we have heard in the course of the various lectures given here this winter, which may be taken as a continuation of the lectures on St. Luke's and St. Matthew's Gospels and of what was given here with reference to the lectures on St. John's Gospel which I gave in Stockholm. From the way in which these lectures were given, it will be clear that there never was any question in a narrow sense of explaining the Gospels, but rather that from the truths which in the first place are truths in themselves and as such can be found in the Gospels if rightly understood, light can be thrown in different ways upon other riddles of life.

When we go back beyond the founding of Christianity, we find two different kinds of Initiation : that of the North, described in more detail in the above-mentioned Stockholm Lectures, and that of the South, the chief characteristic of which is its connection with the Egyptian methods of Initiation. In the world of the ancients there were two different methods by which they could penetrate into the Spiritual world. In old Egypt a candidate for initiation had to descend into the depths of his own soul, beyond all that plays its part in the ordinary soul-life, as thinking, feeling and willing, and the like. There he found that from which the soul itself came forth : the divine Spiritual life of the world. A descent beneath those regions of the soul which are illuminated and permeated by the Ego, was the essential point in the Egyptian, or indeed, in any southern Initiation. In the Northern Initiation, on the other hand, the object striven for was that man should come out of himself, and expand into the phenomena of the world in a state of ecstasy. This was especially the case in the Germanic Druidic Mysteries and those of the Trotten. We heard how these two kinds of Initiation were combined in one stream, in what we call the Christian Initiation, and how this represented a higher unity combining the ecstatic Initiation of the North with the mystical contraction of the South. This gives an indication of a deeper foundation of cosmic Mysteries, permeating all existence. In reality this is in itself as great and mighty a fact as the fusion of the two different forms of Initiation of ancient times into the one single form of Christian Initiation ; it is an example of a great and still more comprehensive law permeating all human existence, and also interwoven in the existence of all the outer world-phenomena, in so far as these are known to man. Everywhere we find ourselves confronted by opposites, by two parts of a duality. The Northern and Southern initiations offer one example of two opposite sides—

polarities, as we might call them—that confront us in the life of the world. The other, the Christian initiation—in which these two forms of initiation flow together and as it were celebrate a Spiritual marriage—is an example of how opposites, dualities of any sort, reunite. This takes place without cessation ; unities are always separating into dualities for the purpose of furthering evolution, while dualities unite again, and once more form unities. We can point externally to one great and mighty fact, extending beyond human evolution, which is an example of this division of unity into a duality, and of the streaming back of the two into one.

We have often thrown light on the Lemurian Epoch, which experienced, among other things, that great fact in the evolution of the world, the separation of the Moon from our Earth. That epoch also saw the first beginnings of that which in the present day sense of man's development, we may call the two opposites : man and woman ; whereas in the ages preceding that of Lemuria we should only find unity of sex. There was an original unity, which separated into man and woman. We have already indicated, moreover, that in a future age the two sexes will once more become one, that the duality will again become a unity, a unity will come forth from a duality. That is the external indication of a far-reaching series of facts connected with the relation of two to one, or one to two.

What we thus meet with in the development of mankind is actually the expression, the image, of a still greater cosmic polarity rooted in a unity ; greater than the example in our present-world life, of the two that in a distant future will be fused into one. It is necessary that we should take every one of the thoughts given us by Spiritual Science in its full depths, not allowing ourselves to form a habit of taking such thoughts in the same superficial way as other thoughts and conceptions which prevail in the world to-day, and which our present civilisation in its hasty and superficial triviality accepts. The thoughts of Spiritual Science must be taken as earnestly as possible. Therefore such a thought as that often spoken of and which indeed underlies all our teaching —that man as a little world, as a microcosm, is born out of the Macrocosm, the great world—must not simply be taken as an abstract thought, for in its content it is manifold and infinite. Above all, we must realise that the world contains more depth than is supposed ; and that even when we have grasped a polarity or a truth in one of its aspects, that does not by any means signify that we know the last truth about it ; rather must we patiently wait and observe, so that when we know one side of a thing, we should try to learn what refers to the other side of it.

Man is born out of the whole Cosmos ; he must look up it to as to his Father-Mother, of whom he himself is an image. Yes, man is an image of the whole world with which he is acquainted, there is nothing in the being of man which does not in some way relate to what can be found in the great Cosmos. If we compare man, as seen to-day in the light of Spiritual Science, with the human forms of early ages, we find among others one characteristic feature of immense importance for the understanding of the nature of man. This sign can teach every one of us that, as regards what we have known about the world, the fact that some things that have been said are true, is not of sole importance ; there is something else besides, something very different. When a man has proved the truth of a thing, he has not even then told us what is of greatest importance in it. For example, there is much truth in what a trivial natural scientist will tell about the resemblance between man and the higher mammals. It is an indisputable truth that man has the same number of bones and muscles, and so on. But after this has been proved, the last word on the subject has not been said. Man must learn, through the deepening and inwardness of Spiritual Science, to acquire a feeling for the value of a particular truth, to sense whether or no it is important and essential for the elucidation of a matter. People come along to-day and speaking from their trivial consciousness, keep on assuring us of the truth of their assertions. We have no wish to contradict them. But the point is, of what value are they for the understanding of the world ? Now there is a certain fact—which is undeniably true, and with which everyone is acquainted, because we meet with it over and over again every day—the value of which, in its significance to man should be realised and felt in the right way. That is, the fact that man stands and walks upright and can gaze out into space around him. Man alone is capable of that ! For we must say that even though the apes look as though they might possess this power, they have somehow missed it, for they cannot walk upright. Man is the only being who has achieved this, and who has succeeded in raising his countenance freely into the space around him. This fact is immeasurably more important than all those that a trivial Natural Science tells us as to the position occupied by man among the animals. What science says is true, but this is of much greater importance. If we wish to feel the force of this, we must make ourselves acquainted with the reason why man is a being that walks upright, a being certainly still bound to the earth, but one who, through his mental outlook and even through his sense-perceptions, raised himself into an upright position in space. The reason is that there is a certain polarity, a duality in the Cosmos, which corresponds to another duality in man. We can point to a duality in the universe and to a duality in man, as two opposites, existing in the microcosm and the macrocosm. The one alluded to in the macrocosm, in the great world, is that of the Sun to the Earth ; and the same polarity that exists between Sun and Earth exists also in man. It is that between his head and his hands and feet ; between his head and his limbs. As time goes on these things will be gone into more fully, but we must in the first place make ourselves acquainted with them and learn to feel that in a certain respect the head and limbs of man bear the same relation to each other as the Sun does to the Earth in our solar System. There are, in fact, in our earth those forces which in the course of the ages have brought about the whole form and movement of our hands and feet through certain mysterious forces which bind man to the Earth ; while the forces which have lifted his countenance up in space, and which have transformed him from a being which gazes on to the earth to one who can look out into the infinite distances of cosmic space,—these forces have their seat in the Sun. Anyone who really has the right feeling will have the same impression when contemplating the self-evident polarity between man's head and his limbs, as he will if he turns his attention to the polarity between the Sun and Earth. This polarity will some day become a unity in the life of man, just as the Cosmic polarity will do.

Even as the Sun and Earth were once a single being which later divided into a duality, so will they some day be re-united ; and the polarity in man between head and limbs will also some day become unity, difficult to imagine as it may seem to the man of to-day, who is not accustomed to such concepts.

We have thus pointed to a polarity in man and to its correspondence in the universe. There are, however, other polarities in man, which also have their corresponding counterparts in the universe. As regards the polarity between the head and limbs, all human beings on the earth are alike. It exists equally in man and woman. In this respect there is no difference between them ; for every other polarity, for example that in the configuration of the soul, is not affected by this. If there were no other polarity but that existing between the microcosm and macrocosm, man and woman would be alike, but as it is they form another polarity in the being of man. Now we may ask : can we not also find a polarity in the universe corresponding to that between man and woman in human life ? That can be found too. But before we are able to look for it we must make ourselves to some slight extent acquainted, in an occult sense, with the polarity between man and woman. In so doing we must not fall into the error of our materialistic age, which applies the polarity between man and woman—taking it simply as a question of sex—to the whole universe. Not only is that a trivial thing to do, but our learned men are taking a liberty when they consider that what is found in one domain is applicable to every other.

The corresponding polarity in the universe to that existing on our earth between man and woman cannot be called male and female. That would be nonsense. We must investigate the occult foundations of this other polarity. The polarity between male and female in our earthly evolution does not, of course, apply to the ' human being.' The human being as such is the same in both man and woman. When we speak of man and woman we only refer to the configuration of their physical and etheric bodies. This has nothing to do with the inner being of man ; so that we cannot, in an occult sense, speak as our materialistic age does. A man and woman each possesses an astral body and an ego, but the ordinary perception knows nothing of that which makes a man or woman a human being, it can only speak of them as it sees them. We are not now speaking of the human being as such in man or woman, but of what constitutes a man or a woman, which is merely their outer sheaths. This must be thoroughly understood ; for if what is about to be said were to be applied to the human being as such, it would be completely wrong. The polarity between man and woman within the above-named limits is as follows :—

In primeval ages the external human form was totally different. The present human forms—male and female—have gradually evolved out of an earlier single form, which had not yet divided into two. There was formerly a unity, where now there is a polarity, between man and woman. Now we know too, that the earlier uni-form was of a finer, more spiritual kind. Only in the course of ages did man develop a dense material form. When we look back not only do we find uni-form, but one which was more spiritual than the human form to-day. We have a primeval human being neither man nor woman, unity as yet undivided, and finer, more etheric, more spiritual than the later and more material human being, now separated into man and woman. What was the cause of the original unity having later developed into Man and Woman ? This cause came about because, when the unity became a duality, the woman formed a physical body for herself which, if we may say such a thing, did not completely pass from the earlier form into the normal material form. The body of woman remained at a more spiritual stage, it did not fully descend into the material. It has certainly become dense and material, but at the same time it has retained an earlier, more spiritual form. Thus a spiritual stage has become material. The body of woman has, as it were, retained an earlier, more spiritual form, which has not descended completely into matter. Though it has become material, it has not done so as regards its form, for it still retains the form the human being originally possessed. Hence we may say : Woman is a manifestation of an earlier formation which was intended to be Spiritual and which, as seen to-day, is actually false, a maya, an illusion. If we accept the idea of a certain point in evolution when a spring-forward was made and when matter was crystallised, we can say : the woman did not press forward as far as that point, she crystallised an earlier form. To one who can really perceive the facts of life, or who learns them through imaginative cognition, a woman's body is a somewhat truer imprint of the Spiritual behind it only as far as the head and limbs are concerned, that is to say, that her head and limbs alone express in their material appearance, something of a resemblance to their spiritual counterpart. The Spiritual behind the material form does not look like that, because the latter is not a true form.

Thus the saying that the world is ' Maya ' can be applied to every region of life. It is very easy simply to state that ' the world is Maya,' but a man cannot grasp its meaning, if he does not go seriously into it, inquiring : ' In how far are forms illusion ' ? Some are more so and others less. There are those which at any rate approximately do in their outer semblance express the Spiritual behind them ; these are the head and limbs. Others there are which are completely wrong and out of drawing ; to these belong the rest of the human body, which is quite out of drawing. When the world understands these things it will no longer speak as foolishly as it does to-day, for it will then see that a certain deep, yet more delicate artistic sense tells us that the female form, with the exception of the head and limbs, is out of drawing, and if it is to be artistically represented the defects must be corrected. In better and more artistic times this was actually done, for no one who really has an eye for form can fail to observe that in the Venus of Milo the form has to a certain extent been corrected ; but this as a rule is not noticed.

In this way we have divided the human being into two parts, consisting of those members of the body which are less of an illusion and those others that are more so and quite out of drawing. This does not apply to woman alone ; but where a man is concerned the whole thing is reversed. He is the opposite pole. Just as the female form did not descend so far as the normal point necessary for rightly expressing the spirit in matter but crystallised at an earlier stage, so the male body on the other hand sprang just as far beyond that normal point as the female form stopped short of it. Thus the male body descended more deeply than the normal into materiality, and manifests this in its outer form. It would have quite a different appearance if it had not sprung beyond the middle point. Only as regards the head and limbs does the human body even approximately correspond to truth. As regards the rest of its form we must say that the female body, having reached a certain point, remained at a standstill ; it consolidated before the waves of material existence broke over it ; hence it manifests quite a different form from that which we should have seen if it had but waited till it had come in contact with material life before crystallising. The male body on the other hand plunged too deeply down and is just as greatly out-of-drawing as that of woman. Thus the woman's body manifests a distorted form in the Spiritual, while the man's body is distorted in the material. The true form would be between the two ; it would consist of a happy average of both. Of course this affects the whole human being in his earth-life, in so far as he has a physical covering. What I have just said has nothing to do with the polarity between the head and limbs, it refers to the whole human being in one incarnation between birth and death. We incarnate either as man or woman. In so doing we have to take into account that which is out-of-drawing in the man or woman ; but that extends to the whole human being, and the consequence is that if in one incarnation one has the body of a woman, the whole of this female body is influenced by the fact of its having remained behind at an earlier stage when the form was more pliable. In a male incarnation the whole physical body is permeated with the effects of having plunged down too strongly into coarse solid matter. If people had even the smallest inkling of what it means to think in the spirit, to live in the spirit, using the physical body only as an instrument,—so that one does not feel firmly fastened into it, identifying oneself with it—they would sing psalms about the misery of having to use a male body in an incarnation, for of course these material effects have also filtered into the brain. One observes that the forms of the male brain, through having been deeper into matter, are more difficult to manage than the more flexible forms of the female brain. It is truly a more difficult matter to train a male brain for the ascent into the higher worlds, and to translate the truths into thoughts, than it is to train a female brain for the same purpose. For this reason it is not surprising to people who think, when a new conception of the world arises such as that of Spiritual Science, it is more easily grasped by the more manageable female brain ; for it is more difficult for the male brain, being less pliable and obedient, to free itself from certain thoughts which it has absorbed. Hence Spiritual Science will not find an easy acceptance amongst the men who are to-day the leaders of culture and of the cultured ideas prevalent in our day. We must realise how awkward an instrument is the brain of a learned man to-day, not only for the acceptance of Spiritual Science, but also for thinking along those lines. But we must not look at these things in a wrong way and draw our own conclusions—rather should we look upon it as all the more significant that there are so many men whose brains are so pliant that they have become intimately acquainted with Spiritual Science.

These things can at first merely be hinted at, but if you allow them to work on you and then reflect over them, you will find immense perspective opening out regarding the life of man.

When we think of human life in its two opposites of man and woman, we are confronted with two forms, one that has remained at a standstill at an earlier stage, and one which has jumped on beyond the present stage and which draws into the present a form intended for the future, but presents it as a caricature. The female has preserved an earlier form and the male has taken on a later form, but has made it what it must not be in the future. The male form is incorrect, because it has brought later conditions of life into an age as yet too early for them.

Can we find a correspondence in the Cosmos to the polarity between male and female. Is there anything in the Cosmos which on the one hand shows us a development which has retained earlier forms and carried these over into a later age? And are there on the other hand forms which have transcended a certain stage, thus representing the caricatured form of a future state? If we bring to mind the concrete development which we know from the Akashic Records, we may put the question thus: Is there anything in the Cosmos outside, resembling an old Moon-existence which would not enter the Earth-existence, but retained from the old Moon something feminine in the Cosmos?

Is there anything which carries into the present time something like an old Moon existence belonging to an earlier stage? And is there in the Cosmos anything which has gone beyond a certain stage, and has condensed and thickened, so that it represents a later condition, a Jupiter condition?

There is! There is in the Cosmos the same polarity as we have described between male and female; and that is the polarity between a Comet and the Moon. If we wish to understand the nature of a Comet, wandering as it does in cosmic space regardless of the other laws of the Solar System, we must be clear as to the fact that the Comet carries the laws belonging to the old Moon-existence into our own. Those laws it has preserved, and with those it enters our existence. It has taken on the present substance of the solar-terrestrial system; but, as regards its motion and its nature, it has remained behind at that stage of natural law which prevailed in the Solar System when our earth was still Old Moon. It carries a former condition into a later, into the present; just as the woman's body carries an earlier condition into present-day existence. The nature of the Comet is one part of a polarity, and that of the Moon represents the other pole. When, in the Lemurian age the Moon evolved out of the Earth, it took with it certain portions, which had to be removed in order that the human being as such might develop. The earth was not to become as dense as it must have become if it had retained the Moon within it. The Moon actually represents a caricature of the Jupiter-condition. Just as a fresh ripe fruit is found in a petrified state in a stalactite, so the Moon in its configuration transcended the middle form, as has the male form of the human being. Exactly the same polarity that we find in human life between the male and the female, we can find in the Cosmos between the natures of Moon and Comets.

Thus are these things connected: as sun to earth, so head to limbs,—as Moon to Comet, so man to woman in the human being. Here again we must not go home and say:—well, now, we have some nice polarities to observe!— We must take these things very seriously and remember that on other occasions I said something more besides this. We must take into consideration the fact that a man is only male as regards his physical body, for as regards his etheric body he is female ; and the woman on the other hand is only female in her physical body. A woman can only be said to be female as far as her physical body is concerned and that can be said of the etheric body of a man ; so that the relation of the etheric body of a man to the etheric body of a woman is as that of Comet to Moon. If you like you may perhaps say : this makes every-thing confused again ! But these things are so. In a culture which has created its ideas with a densified brain, those same ideas tend to create dense outlines which cannot be modified, so that when ideas are once formed they must be held on to. But the spirit does not admit of this. That is mobile, and when we form ideas, we must keep them plastic. So we must apply what has just been said as to the relation of the Moon and Comets to Man and Woman, to the male in the woman and the female in the man. It applies to the male and female elements in the human being but not to man and woman as we meet them externally.

We have now found some extremely interesting connections between the development of the human being and that of the Cosmos. Of course, as I have already observed : Those who sit in the high places of ' true scientific observa-tion ' will consider what has just been put forward about the Comet and the Moon, as utterly wild and absurd. That cannot be helped. They do not desire to investigate the truth. But on the ground of Spiritual Science, we can build a bridge between that which comes from the Spiritual and what is seen on the physical plane. Those others will not do this.

In the year 1906, during the Congress in Paris, I called attention to the fact that Spiritual investigation from its knowledge of the nature of Comets, was able to say : As the combinations of carbon and hydrogen play the same part on our earth as did the combinations of carbon and nitrogen (cyanogen) on the Old Moon, the cometary life must contain cyanogen compounds,—combinations of carbon and nitrogen. Those persons who have followed these things atten-tively will remember this. Our Spiritual Science, therefore, some time ago announced that the cometary nature must contain cyanogen in some form. During the last few weeks this fact has been mentioned in all the newspapers as an external fact discovered by spectro-analysis. This is only one case—hun-dreds of others could be quoted—in which Spiritual investigation builds bridges for the facts of external research. In this case spectro-analysis asserts what Spiritual Science stated years before. The results of external material-istic investigation never contradict those of Spiritual research. We may depend upon statements such as the above-mentioned, when those who sit in the high places of true science constantly point to the external facts. Only we must not confuse these facts with the limited conclusions which people draw for themselves. If everything in Natural Science to-day was really a fact, Natural Science would greatly contradict Spiritual Science ; but their facts are no facts, only the corrupt conceptions of those who, through the conditions pre-vailing in our age, are called upon to deal with such matters.

Now, having brought before our minds the polarity to be found in human life as well as in the Cosmos, we may ask : What then is brought forth from the Universe as a result of this ?

It is rather difficult to describe in a somewhat short time the immensity underlying such a fact. You will allow me, therefore, by way of example, to describe the life of man as it runs its course seen externally. First of all, we see something of which we may say, it pursues its course like the life of a good citizen, from day to day. He gets up in the morning, eats his breakfast and completes the rest of the day in accordance with the usual rules. There are certain events, however, which can intervene in a man's life at one fell swoop, and may bring about changes in the day's course. Take the case of a man and wife living for a while the life of good citizens with but little variety in the usual programme of their day, till something occurs which actually causes a leap in the ordinary external life of people in such circumstances. When a new human being incarnates, and enters life as a citizen of the world, the event causes a leap, a great change in the ordinary process of everyday life. When a new citizen of the world comes on the horizon of man and wife, something actually occurs which gives the whole family connection a new form. I brought this forward as an example by means of which we can gain some little understanding of the deep occult background of cometary life. In the Cosmos too, life goes on from day to day, from year to year—like the life of the good citizen—one day is like another ; the Sun rises and sets, the plants blossom in spring, and wither away in autumn, and when there is rain or sunshine or hail or the like, these correspond to such events in ordinary life as, for instance, when instead of our ordinary five o'clock tea, we have a little party. We see these things happening as a matter of course. All this hangs together with the laws underlying the movements of Sun, earth, and so on, and the way in which these continue day by day and year by year. Into this regular process, there intervenes the rarer, yet in a certain respect recurrent, appearances of the comets. They come upon the process of Cosmic happenings like a new citizen entering the horizon of man and wife. Through the appearance of a comet in the cosmos, something is actually brought about in the life of humanity which could not occur in the ordinary process of life. If evolution is to continue, there must be, not only that which repeats itself day by day, but something new must be introduced into it. Just as something quite special enters the life of a family with the birth of a new earth-citizen, so something quite different enters the progress of the human race on earth through the appearance of a comet, which breaks through the ordinary process of cosmic existence. It is actually as though something new were born, when a comet appears.

One who can investigate these things spiritually is able to indicate quite definitely the different functions of the separate comets, and how each one has to introduce something spiritually new into the world. Thus Halley's comet is one of those which, in its periodic appearances, always introduces something specially new into the life of man. Whereas otherwise things recur in the ordinary way, this comet brings about a new birth in human inner life and culture. I can only characterise what I mean, by referring to the three last appearances of Halley's comet, in the years 1759, 1835, and the one we are now expecting. What are the tasks of these three appearances ? Other comets have other tasks. New births in the universe are not always to be greeted with the same joy as the birth of a young citizen into a family. All sorts are born into the universe ; those that bring humanity forward as well as those that drive it back. Now the appearance of Halley's comet, or what it signifies spiritually for the further evolution of humanity, is connected with that which humanity had to absorb out of the Cosmos at the various periods of Kali-Yuga in order that thought should descend more and more into materiality. With every new appearance of this comet a new impulse was born, to drive humanity further away from a spiritual cosmic conception by the Ego, and to urge it to grasp the world in a more materialistic way. This does not mean a descent into matter, but rather the driving of that Spiritual substance which the human Ego should draw from the universe for its Spiritual existence, down into the sphere of materialistic conception. All those conceptions of the second half of the 18th century, which are called shallow and superficial and which Goethe so ridiculed in his *Truth and Poetry* and which found their exponent for instance in Holbach's *Système de la Nature*, are understood in their cosmic sense through the appearance of Halley's comet in the year 1759. The commonplace materialistical literature of the second third of the 19th century was preceded by the appearance of that comet in 1835. Things that take place microcosmically on the earth are macrocosmically connected with events of the great world. A new impulse towards materialism was again given by the appearance of Halley's comet in 1835. Büchner, Vogt and Moleschott are examples of those who were influenced on the earth by what appeared with Halley's comet, as a mighty sign from the Cosmos. We are now to be confronted in the near future—for humanity must be tested, must rise out of itself, must feel the resistance to Spirituality so that it may unfold all the more forces for its re-ascent—we shall be confronted with the forces which the new appearance of this comet will send forth from the universe, forces which may lead humanity down into a still more arid and dreadful materialism. Something may be born, which even the most arid and driest thoughts of the Büchner school could not have imagined. But this possibility is a necessity, for only if man overcomes the opposing forces can he acquire the strong force able to lead him up again.

If we bear this in mind, we shall then encounter in the right way what we call ' Signs from the Heavens.' This is really a fact; though what I have said must not be taken in a superstitious sense, as though God were pointing with a wand from Heaven to show men what they have to do ! The approaching appearance of Halley's comet is one of these signs, and notice should be taken of it. For a mighty ascending impulse must follow it that we may rise from the depths of materialism into which we have sunk, into Spirituality. Just as we are given the possibility of being swamped in materialism, we are also given the chance to ascend into clearer, spiritual heights.

It was clearly and distinctly indicated in the last lectures that during the first half of the 20th century an etheric clairvoyance will develop in a few single individuals, as a natural capacity. In order that man may not sink more deeply into the materialism indicated by the present sign of 1910, those who have understanding of Spiritual Science have the possibility of developing those forces in the human soul which can lead man beyond materialism. If a man understands these forces, they will teach him how he may himself see the etheric nature of Christ. We are living at an important crossing-point, when men will be taught, even by signs from heaven, that in one direction the path will lead deeper into the mire, while the other path leads to the development in themselves of the forces which, at the conclusion of Kali-Yuga, will lead to etheric clairvoyance. The cry of John the Baptist : ' Change the disposition of your souls,' applies to us to-day ! This may really be said. Just as on the one hand we are given the possibility of perishing in the materialistic morass, on the other it is possible, through the Sun reaching a certain point in the Constellation of Pisces at the Vernal Equinox, that a certain etheric clairvoyance may be acquired. For the spiritual ascent there are also signs, to show us how the forces come from the Cosmos. If a man is a student of Spiritual Science he will of necessity grow to understand this decision ; if he does not, that means that he has not understood Spiritual Science aright. We must pass through the test submitted to us by the sign in the Heavens which we now recognise to be the appearance of Halley's Comet.

Let us now picture the vision of Christ, as it will appear to the first forerunners during the next 2,500 years, and as it appeared to Paul on the way to Damascus. Man will ascend to a cognition of the spiritual world and will see the physical world permeated by a new ' country,' or new realm. Man's physical environment will present a totally different aspect in the course of the next 2,500 years, through the addition of an etheric realm, which indeed is already here now, but which he will learn to perceive. This etheric sphere is even now spread out before the eyes of those who have carried their esoteric training as far as ' Illumination '—as was the case with the Initiates even in Kali-Yuga. That which men will see more and more in the future is visible in its greatest heights to the Initiates. The Initiate draws from thence at repeated intervals, the forces he requires. When he has to carry out some special work, he draws his forces from those realms within the earth's circuit which are visible to him, but which can only be seen by those who have the vision. It will help us to understand this, when we know that a part of that land from which the Initiate drew his forces during Kali-Yuga, will be thrown open to a great part of humanity during the next 2,500 years. Formerly, in the days of primeval clairvoyance, man, though then without the strong Ego-consciousness, could see into the Spiritual world—and in a way he saw more or less what he will see now,—but he will now enter it with his newly acquired self-consciousness. At that time he saw it in dream-like ecstatic conditions, or by looking into his own soul. That world which during Kali-Yuga became physical was then open to man's gaze. Hence the traditions, which have preserved recollections of the old clairvoyance, tell us of an unknown Fairy-Land which has now disappeared from sight. There are wonderful documents in Eastern literature full of a peculiar tragical enchantment, and telling us that at one time it was possible for human beings to travel to a land where the Spiritual flowed into the physical. It is that Land from whence at certain times the Initiates—and at all times the Bodhisattvas—drew fresh forces. The Eastern writings speak with deep sorrow of that land, asking : ' Where is it ? We are told the names of places, paths are named ; but the Land itself is concealed, even from those most initiated among the Lamas of Thibet ! ' Only to the highest Initiates is it accessible. But it is always stated that some day this Land will return to earth. That is true ; it will return to earth ! And the guide thereto will be He Whom

62

men will see, when, through the vision of the Event of Damascus, they reach the Land of Shamballa. 'Shamballa'—for so this Land is called—has withdrawn from the sight of man. It can only be entered to-day by those who, as Initiates, go there from time to time to be strengthened. The old forces can no longer lead man thither. That is why Eastern literature speaks with such tragic despair of the vanished Land of Shamballa. But the Christ-Event, which will be vouchsafed to man in this century through his newly-awakened faculties, will bring back the Fairy-Land of Shamballa, which through the whole of Kali-Yuga could only be known to the Initiates.

Thus humanity is now called upon to make a decision, whether it shall allow itself, through what comes with the Halley Comet, to be led down into a darkness even lower than that of Kali-Yuga, or whether through an understanding developed by Anthroposophy it shall not neglect to cultivate the new faculties by which it may find the way to the Land which according to Eastern Literature has disappeared, but which Christ will once more reveal to mankind; —the Land of Shamballa. That is the great question of the dividing of the ways : either to go down or to go up. Either to go down into something which, as a Cosmic-Kamaloka lies still deeper down than Kali-Yuga, or to work for that which will enable man to enter that realm, which is really alluded to under the name of Shamballa.

———

LECTURE 6.

THE BIRTH OF CONSCIENCE.

Berlin, 2nd May, 1910.

In the course of the lectures given here last winter we considered the Being of Christ from many different aspects and we endeavoured in various ways to point out that what we know as the Christ-Impulse is the most powerful factor for the development of mankind that we have ever possessed in the whole evolution of the earth. It is therefore easy to understand that, in the first place, this subject can never be exhausted, that there could be no end to all one might do to elucidate further the Christ-Impulse from all sides, and moreover, when all is said and done, all that is of profoundest interest to man is really connected with the appearance of Christ. We saw that the Gospels themselves attempted to approach the subject of the Being of Christ from four different sides, and we touched upon several of the secrets contained in the different Gospels. We were only able up to a certain point to throw light on that of St. Matthew. It must be left for the present, and we shall return to the secrets of St. Matthew's Gospel in lectures to be given at a later time, after which we can venture further into the depths of St. Mark's Gospel. If we were now, at the conclusion of our winter lectures in this group, to give more sketchy indications of what remains to be discussed, it would interfere with the harmony of the lectures to be given later. To-day, as also in our next lecture, we shall touch upon questions which in a certain respect relate to the Christ-Problem ; in fact, we shall to-day refer to the question of the connection between the human conscience and the intervention of the Christ-Impulse in the development of mankind. In so doing we also achieve another object. Next Thursday the public Lectures on 'The Human Conscience' will be given, and we shall speak on that same subject in our group-meeting to-day. There is a definite purpose in this—one which, as time goes on, will often be apparent to our Spiritual vision. The object is to show that the same subject can be spoken of in a different way in a study-group such as this, from the way in which it must be handled in a public lecture, intended for persons who are not members of our movement. The Anthroposophist, among many other capacities which he must acquire, must also acquire a feeling of how matters concerning the world can be approached from many standpoints and from many different sides, and that a man who has already mastered certain basic facts can both speak and hear of a subject in a different way from one who has not. When we speak in a study-group we assume that the minds of those present have to some extent become accustomed to the conceptions of a Spiritual world, that as regards their thoughts and feelings they are already in that world and are therefore able, by means of those thoughts and feelings, to form a concept of the human conscience. The answer to such questions can be drawn from much greater depths in a study-group than in a public lecture given to a non-Anthroposophical audience. Those public lectures have indeed the mission, by means of the phenomena of the soul-life,—introduced in the first place as external experience,—of giving a sort of proof that the truths known to Spiritual Science are truths indeed. That is a different task for the Spiritual Scientist, who probably brings with him certain inner convictions and perhaps even certain opinions about the Spiritual world. He must gradually learn to become acquainted with ideas and concepts from all sorts of different sources and sides which will help him to make certain things clear, and he must leave off looking at things and speaking of them in one way only, though that method, of course still prevails in external life.

The question of the human conscience is one that must stir the very depths of our souls. For centuries philosophers and thinkers the whole world over, have been more interested in this subject than in any other. With regard to the phenomenon of conscience one might easily succumb to the illusion—which has often been here described as such—of believing that everything to be found in the human soul to-day, was always to be found there. Yet, as we know, the various soul-faculties and processes which man has developed in the course of thousands of years, were very different in primeval times from what they are now. Much of what is now most prized and valued in our soul-life, we did not possess when we wandered on earth thousands of years ago, in other incarnations. There is a purpose in these many incarnations of ours, as we have often emphasised. The purpose is that the soul should in the course of its development from one incarnation to another, acquire ever-new capacities and forces ; that it should have a history of its own ; that its earth-existence should be a time of learning to realise that the soul was not the same when our incarnations just began as it is now, and that moreover in the distant future it will again be different. The human conscience too,—that precious possession of the human soul, which speaks like the voice of God in each individual man or woman, warning them of good or evil—even this precious gift was not always in man's inner being. Conscience, too, is something that has developed. And indeed it is not so very long ago, comparatively speaking, that the human conscience announced its presence, since when it has developed more and more. Yet precious as this possession is to us, it is not intended that it should continue to live in the human soul in all the ages yet to come, just in its present form. It will develop further, and take different forms ; it will discover itself as something which man had to acquire, and which will bear fruit. And in later ages, when these fruits are his, it will be something upon which man can look back, saying : There once was a time when, in the course of my passage through the different incarnations, I was able to embody into my soul that which is now my conscience, and I am now enjoying the fruits of that ! Just as we now look back at a time when our souls were in other incarnations and did not possess what we call conscience, so in later times our souls will look back at the present time and exclaim : Hail to that past ! Thanks for the gifts which in the past became our human conscience ! If we had not then been able to develop a human conscience in our souls, we should now lack what we need for our present life !

From this we see that conscience forms part of the treasures of the soul at the present time, and if we understand something of the nature and being of the human conscience it gives us a sort of understanding of our age, and of its psychic life. Man's conscience came into being; that is a fact we have often referred to in various connections. In the public lecture next Thursday I shall state that one can, as it were, point to the very time when conscience was first discovered in the human soul. If we go back a few centuries into ancient Greece, about five hundred years before the Christian era, we come to the great poet, Æschylos. When we let the personages depicted by the mighty genius of the old Greek dramatist work upon us, we do not find what is to-day called conscience, or at any rate not designated by that name. Five hundred years before the Christian era the greatest dramatist then existing had no words to express what we now call the human conscience. If he wanted to express that process in the human soul which corresponds to what we now call conscience, he had to do so in this way :—If a man committed the sin of murdering his mother, he was, through the might of the event made to see into the Spiritual worlds and there he perceived certain figures, which were known to the ancient Greek as the Erinyes and later to the Romans as the Furies. Thus, according to Æschylos, a man who had committed the evil deed of murdering his mother, did not, as he would to-day, hear the reproachful voice of conscience in his inner being; but something drove him to spiritual vision, and he saw around him figures, the avengers of his deed.

This is one of the remarkable proofs to be found in the historical development of man, of what has just been asserted, that in olden times the capacities of the human soul were quite different. We have repeatedly emphasised that only gradually has the soul developed to its present power of perceiving the physical-sense world through the senses, and of using reason as it is used to-day. We stated that in olden times the soul possessed a certain clairvoyance as a normal capacity. At the time of Æschylos this only appeared in special cases. For instance, it became clairvoyant when it was to see what it had brought about in the physical world by its wrong-doing. The soul of Orestes became clairvoyant after the murder of his mother. He then saw the spirits he had aroused in the spiritual world by his deed. They encompassed his soul on all sides. There was nothing of the nature of conscience in his soul; but a clairvoyant consciousness set in, enabling him to see the disorder brought about in the spiritual world by his wrong-doing. In olden times we find that when an evil deed was accomplished, no voice of conscience was heard, for in those days the soul was in a clairvoyant condition and could see what came about in the external world in consequence of a wrong.

What is it then that occurs when a wrong is done? Something is brought about by ourselves in the spiritual world. It is a purely materialistic belief that a wrong can take place without anything taking place in the spiritual world; it produces quite definite processes therein,—effects radiate from us which, though invisible to sense perception can be clearly seen by spiritual sight. These spiritual processes, radiating from one who has done wrong, provide nourishment for certain Spiritual beings who are actually present in the spiritual world. Such beings cannot approach man at all times; they can only do so when the radiations resulting from evil actions emanate from him. It is just the same as with a room—if it is quite clean no flies will enter it ; there are no flies in a perfectly clean room ; but if food is left about or dirt of any kind, the flies come immediately—. So, the moment a man radiates certain spiritual emanations as a result of his evil action, he is surrounded by beings who feed on them. These are the beings whom Æschylos, the great Greek dramatist, depicts around Orestes. What we to-day know as the inner voice, Æschylos represented in external forms because he was so conscious of it ; for he knew that in special cases, a certain clairvoyant consciousness which was formerly the common possession of all men, could still be aroused. There is always something remaining in later times of what existed previously, but it appears atavistically, and only in abnormal cases. No blame should attach to Shakespeare for representing something of the nature of an objective conscience.

We need only trace Greek Art a little further, from Æschylos to Euripedes, who in his tragedies shows us that he already had the idea of conscience. In ancient Greece we can see how the idea of conscience gradually came into being during the last five hundred years before Christ. Look where you will in the old Testament for a word corresponding to what we to-day call conscience : you will not find one. Conscience, as a quality, drew into the human soul ; and if, instead of contemplating short spans of time we look at great periods, we see that conscience entered the human soul at about the same time as the Christ Impulse. We might say that conscience followed close on the Christ Impulse ; it entered the historical development of the world almost like the shadow of that Impulse. In order to understand this, we must call to mind much that we have learned in the course of past years and make it fruitful for our understanding of what the human conscience really is.

If we wish in a deeper sense to grasp what conscience is, we must call to mind that particular period of time during which mankind in the course of its development was approaching the Christ Impulse and in which it absorbed this Impulse, and then gradually passed into our own, when development proceeded further. We know that this includes three epochs of civilisation in the development of man, which we designate as the Egyptian-Chaldean, the Græco-Latin and our present period. (The two epochs preceding these we may for the moment leave out of consideration ; for our own souls were then too far removed from the possibility of having even an inkling of what we mean to-day by the concept of conscience.) In the Egyptian-Chaldean civilisation we see a gradual preparation of everything which subsequently rose to the greatest height possible, so that in the Graeco-Latin civilisation it might be able to reach and absorb the significant impulse we know as the Christ Impulse. And in our own age we see the epoch in which this Impulse will be further developed, and this will be continued increasingly in the epoch still to come. Now, if we recollect more closely the development of man from the Egyptian-Chaldean epoch, through the Graeco-Latin, into our own, it is clear that in each of these epochs one part of the human soul was developed. Of these, what we know as the Sentient Soul was developed during the Egyptian-Chaldean epoch. That, means that we had at one time to be incarnated in Egyptian-Chaldean bodies, so as to be in a position to acquire aright those qualities which serve for the special development of the Sentient Soul. We then as souls, took that quality with us into our next incarnations during the Graeco-Latin epoch, in order then to develop the intellectual or mind-soul, or soul of higher-feeling. And we live in our present incarnations with the fruits of what we gained in that Epoch, so as to be able now, gradually to bring to a higher stage of development, what we call the forces of the Spiritual or Consciousness-soul.[1] So that our souls—as human beings—have been developed throughout these three epochs; and when our own age comes to its conclusion, our souls will then rise to the development of the quality of Spirit-Self. That will come about in the sixth epoch of civilisation. Thus we see, what a profound purpose there is in our going through successive incarnations, namely, that we may gradually acquire these faculties with which we, as human souls, are acquainted,—and in a wider sense acquire those also which extend beyond the mere life of the soul.

Thus, during the Egyptian-Chaldean culture our souls acquired the forces of the Sentient Soul and brought them to their full development;—during the Graeco-Latin age we developed the intellectual soul or soul of higher feeling. Man had to develop in a normal way as far as the intellectual soul; for then only could the Christ-Impulse be exercised upon him.

Now this development took place in quite a different way in different parts of the earth. If we were to allow ourselves to believe, in an easy sort of way, that the development of mankind proceeds in the most simple way possible, we should never arrive at an understanding of that development. One must indeed learn much before one can even to some slight extent grasp the great thoughts of the guiding Cosmic Beings! When man asserts that the truth is simple, that is great arrogance on his part; it shows that he wants to twist the truth to suit his own convenience. It is simply a love of ease which leads him to assert that the truth must be simple. The truth is indeed very complicated, and the spirit of the guiding cosmic beings can only be grasped by us when we make the most intense efforts to plunge into their thoughts, into their most subtle and intimate thoughts. So we ought not to believe that we have exhausted everything, when we say that: our souls have gradually evolved through Egyptian-Chaldean, the Graeco-Roman, and our own epoch. Let us now for a moment transport ourselves to that time when there was as yet no Graeco-Latin, but only Egyptian-Chaldean civilisation.

There were also human beings living then in Greece and in the countries of the Roman Empire; they lived in the countries of the Graeco-Romans before that age began. And in our own countries, on the soil we tread to-day, there were human beings living at the time when the Egyptian-Chaldean civilisation was playing its part in Asia and Africa. While certain souls, in Asia and Africa, at the epoch of the Egyptian-Chaldean period, were more particularly going through all that was to prepare them to receive the Christ-Impulse, others living in the regions of the subsequent Graeco-Latins were preparing to bring something quite different into the collective development of mankind. In our own countries too, there were people living then who were preparing themselves for something else. Not only do our souls take up different

[1] Dr. Steiner has, since 1923, called this the Spiritual Soul.

qualities in successive ages, but during the same age they live together side by side.

In this way different influences are brought to bear on the souls and further complications thus arise in evolution. By this means more is brought into the development of humanity than if everything went along smoothly in a straight line. It is indeed a fact that preparations had to be made in the Graeco-Latin lands, as also in our own, that the right thing might be brought into the development of civilisation from various sides. The Asiatic and African peoples had one mission and the South European peoples another,—while the peoples inhabiting Northern and Central Europe had a different one again. They all had to bring quite different qualities into the collective development of humanity, and they were able to do so because both their gifts and their training were essentially different.

When we turn our gaze towards the Egyptian-Chaldean peoples, to the souls who reached their zenith in that particular age, we must say : These peoples developed certain qualities of the Sentient-Soul, qualities which can be specially developed by the study of the wonderful teachings which then flowed from the sacred centres of Egypt, or from the marvellous astrology which could be learnt in a similar centre in Chaldea. That which flows from the various centres was sent for the very purpose of aiding the soul's progress. The true meaning of what thus flows forth is not to be found in the content of the streams of civilisation, but in what they contribute to the development of the human soul. The content itself passes away ! Only those who in a deeper sense have not all their wits about them can believe otherwise than that in a few centuries of time our contemporary science will just as much have sunk into oblivion, as certain things connected with the Egyptian-Chaldean civilisation have done to-day. Anyone who believes that the Copernican conception of the universe yielded eternal verities, is making a very great mistake ; that will become a thing of the past later on, just as have the discoveries of old Egypt to-day. As far as the content of these things is concerned they pass away, like many another thing in the development of humanity. For instance, in that wonderful picture of the Last Supper by Leonardo da Vinci in Milan, familiar to you all, at any rate in reproduction, there are only faint outlines to be seen to-day ; and we know that before long nothing will remain of the work into which Leonardo da Vinci put his best powers. Some day there will be just as little left of Raphael's works, which so move our souls to-day, when we allow ourselves to be affected by them. All these works of art will perish and there will be no memory of them on the physical plane. The content of these pictures will succumb to death, like the content of the civilisations themselves. But when we stand before these pictures we ought to remember that they flowed out of Raphael's soul, and that his soul was different after he had conjured them forth from what it was before. Thousands and thousands of people who are moved and uplifted by these pictures, are made different through having this experience. And someday, when the whole earth crumbles into dust—as it certainly will,—the external arrangements organised by the various civilisations will no longer exist. But what the souls have acquired will pass over with them into eternity. What the civilisations give us, is given for the advantage of human souls, for into human souls was poured forth what flowed from the Sanctuaries of Egypt and Chaldea and which—for that time—was exalted wisdom. The souls of men were thereby to be brought a step further ; and to the extent that they did advance further, to that extent were they ripe to encounter new treasures, which then, in the Graeco-Latin Age helped the human souls a little further still. If our own souls had not absorbed what they could in the Graeco-Latin Age, they could not now be living into the spiritual soul. That constitutes progress in time.

If we recollect various things said in the public lectures, we are aware that what we call the ' I,' the ego, works in the three soul-principles. Out of the chaos of soul-experiences that we encounter in the Sentient-Soul, Intellectual-Soul and Consciousness- or Spiritual-Soul, the ego gradually develops, crystallising itself therefrom :—but not in the same way in different parts of the earth. For instance, while the souls in Asia and Africa, during the Egyptian-Chaldean Age, had been developed by the influence so long exercised upon them by the revelations of the Chaldean and Egyptian Sanctuaries,—the peoples in Europe who were far removed from these as regards distance, had developed in such a way that they were in a sense ahead of them. In the European countries men had already in a certain sense developed the ego in the Sentient-Soul,—they had developed a strong feeling for the ego.

Here we come to an extremely important point ; those men passed over to Asia and Africa who could wait with their ego until there should have developed in the Sentient-Soul that which was to be the result of the influence of the Egyptian and Chaldean sacred knowledge. Souls were incarnated in the regions subject to this culture, who, more or less without any distinct feeling of the ego-nature, absorbed the sublime teachings and lofty culture. The lofty culture of ancient Chaldea was poured into a Sentient-Soul as yet unconscious of its ego. Here in the North, no such lofty culture was sunk into the soul. It remained more or less uncultivated, but on the other hand, in this very lack, the Sentient-Soul, which had never experienced the warm glow of the revelations pouring in from the Sanctuary knowledge, developed the Consciousness of an ego. We may say that among the peoples of Egypt and Chaldea the ego-consciousness was late in coming, it waited till the Sentient-Soul had absorbed a certain culture and until the later soul-principles had developed. In Europe the ego did not linger, it developed at once in the Sentient-Soul, but on the other hand, it waited till the later soul-principles had been developed before absorbing certain qualities pertaining to the treasures of civilisation. Thus there were certain souls, incarnated in Asia, and Africa, who had hardly any consciousness of their ego but who, in their Sentient-Souls, were granted revelations of a high order ; while in Europe there were souls who, without having any high degree of culture, were able to emphasise their individual ego ; they could both look upon and feel themselves as men, as human individuals. The people of the Greek and Latin countries occupied a middle place between the two extremes and they had the mission of developing the qualities of the Intellectual-Soul. They developed the ego in the Intellectual-Soul,—while at the same time they were also able in that soul to absorb certain forms of civilisation. Thus then, the Egyptian-Chaldean culture waited, holding back the ego for a later time, while the European culture developed it prematurely ; but the Graeco-Latin culture in a sense kept the balance, for it developed a certain civilisation at the same time as the ego.

In this way we can divine a great mystery of our human development, and without knowledge of this we can never understand why the Christ-Impulse could find so unhindered an entrance into Europe and why it gained so much influence there. Why was this ? Could Christ have appeared in Europe ? Might He not have incarnated there in a carnal body ? No ! that would not have been possible. He appeared in the Graeco-Latin Age, that in which the Intellectual-Soul was developed. That age was particularly adapted to come forward to meet Christ, as it were. But Christ could not have made his appearance in Europe, because of the strong ego-feeling prevailing there. This strong, individual feeling of self, was not adapted to produce one single person having the sole prerogative of being able to provide the vehicle for the highest. A premature ego-feeling, a too great feeling of the equality of mankind, had developed in the countries of Europe. It would have been impossible there for one person to tower so greatly above his contemporaries, as did the one who was to provide the vehicle for the Christ. If Christ was to find a body fit for Him to occupy, there must be no premature appearance of the feeling of ' I.' He had, therefore, to appear on the borders of the Egyptian-Chaldean and of the Graeco-Latin culture, where it was possible for a body to be formed not having the premature ego-feeling within it, but having nevertheless the profoundest comprehension of the Spiritual world given by the Egyptian and Chaldean cultures. But if Europe had not the power of preparing a body for the Christ, yet, just because it had prematurely developed the ego in the very dawn of the new life, it had also acquired other faculties, which served—after Christ had appeared—to bring to mankind a full consciousness of the ego, to help men to a full understanding of it. This was possible because the European peoples had acquired the feeling of the ' I ' too early and had as it were grown up with it.

This must be borne in mind if we wish to understand the newer civilisation. In Asia and Africa we find people who know much concerning the world-secrets, and who are skilful in the setting up of certain symbols—who have in fact cultivated their Sentient-Soul in such a way that they have a rich soul-life ; but their Sense of Ego is weak. In Europe we find people who have received less culture through revelations from without ; but on the other hand we find there the type of man who looks to himself, who finds the strongest support in himself. So in Asia the ground was prepared for the coming of Christ, for there a body could be found into which He could draw in,—and in Europe we find the people best prepared to understand the bringer of the ego-consciousness. He brought to the peoples of Europe what they were longing for. Hence it was in Europe that Christian Mysticism was developed, that wonderful Mysticism in which a man sought to draw Christ into his own soul, into his own ego.

Thus the wise guidance of the World prepared mankind in different parts of the earth, so that each epoch of development should find what is right for that time. It is one of the great assets acquired by studying the conception of the world presented by Spiritual Science, that we gain more and more strongly a sense of the wise way in which the development of humanity and of the whole world has been carried on. We see how for thousands of years souls were prepared on the soil of Europe, that they might develop as early as possible a firm centre in their inner being, and for this very purpose they were actually kept back from acquiring the forces so highly evolved in Asia. Therefore, the stream of culture flowed across from Asia, while the strong sense of the personal ego was being developed in Europe. Again, we can actually point out how the Adriatic almost constituted a boundary between a rather weaker sense of self in Greece, where a man did not so much feel himself to be a separate individual as an Athenian, a Spartan, a Theban, a member of his city,—and the Roman culture on the other side, where the strong ego-feeling was developed in the consciousness of the Roman citizen, who stood firmly on his own ground as an individual person. In Greece we still find the ego somewhat of a retiring nature ; man still took in more from the outer world, in such a way that the ego need not be present. If we cross the Adriatic and come to Rome we find the Roman citizen standing firmly on his feet—already conscious of his ego. All this is connected with deep and significant sub-depths. These things do not occur on the physical plane without corresponding events taking place in the Spiritual world. We see that in the culture of Greece there was still a strong influence of the ego that was withheld. Much in Greece was still taken impersonally. The Greek did not feel himself to be a separate citizen, but a member of the organism of Athens, Sparta, or Thebes. This had to be done away with. The longing of man to draw things into himself from without must disappear, and as he becomes more and more a Westerner he must learn to find entrance into the inner part of his soul. What is to be formed by the masses, must be lived and experienced in advance by the Great Leaders, the Great Individualities of humanity. Let us keep before our minds the fact to which we have often referred—that the Greek still had a strong consciousness that what was given him from without, apart from his having greatly developed his inner personality, was of particular value. Once more I would remind you of the saying of a very cultured Greek, which gives us a deep insight into the longings of the Greek people. ' Better be a beggar in the upper world than a king in the realms of shades ! ' The great value of the invisible, of the super-sensible life, had not then been realised. That which could be drawn from the environment without the help of the ego, is drawn from that environment. It is profoundly moving to perceive how at this juncture, at the turning-point of the times, a great Leading Personality stands like a sign-post, to cast off the disposition towards the earlier and to put on the disposition for the new ; to ring forth far and wide, speaking as it were for the spiritual-world: ' A time is now coming when men must no longer take into themselves that which can flow into their personality apart from the ego, but rather that which enters it through the ego ! '

This deed was accomplished by one of the great Sages of ancient Greece ; it was in part fulfilled in Empedokles, in the island of Sicily. In many of the legends which to-day are only told as tales, great depths lie concealed. Empedokles,—the great Sage who was not only a great philosopher but an Initiate into the deep mysteries of his time, who was both one of the greatest statesmen of all times and also a sacrificial priest,—of him the legend (which in an occult sense is true) relates as follows. Having completed his task in Sicily, Empedokles threw his body into Etna, that his external sheaths might be united with the soil of Sicily, thereby to record that 'firm faith in the ego would follow, now that the outer had disappeared !' The sacrifice of the outer sheaths of Empedokles was accomplished when he surrendered them to Etna. There is a deep occult truth behind this. Among the Spiritual experiences in Sicily to-day is the following. If spiritually one breathes the air of Sicily one can still trace in it the after-effects of the deed of Empedokles !—His soul has continued to incarnate ; but his body attained a special significance by having been consciously given over to the elements, so that it can still be found in the spiritual atmosphere of Sicily to-day. The body of Empedokles forms a considerable part of the spiritual atmosphere of Sicily. It was a very important moment to me—such things can be discussed within our groups—when a few days ago I was able to tell our Palermo friends in their actual presence, that if anyone wanders in Sicily with a spiritual consciousness, he certainly still breathes spiritually, even to-day, that which has permeated the air of Sicily ever since the death of Empedokles !

So now we see that the boundary between East and West,—which we, speaking in an external and spatial sense, have referred to as the Adriatic Sea,—was indicated by a great Leader of Humanity, who, as he was to work on further in the West, stripped off the principle by means of which man could grow in the East, desiring to preserve for the future development of man that which is exalted above all the elements of the external physical plane.

It is a very great thing to become aware of these distinctions for they show how, in regions widely separated in space, different effects are being prepared in order that in this variety the greatest may be attained. It is through the co-operative effects of differentiation that the goal of the collective development of mankind must be attained. By this we can see that Christ, after having appeared in the East, went across to the West, there to be accepted by those who were made ready for this by a strong ego-consciousness ; that they might thereby understand the Bringer of that consciousness. That is the secret of Christ's entrance into the West, that He there found souls prepared for Him, and that those souls accepted Him. Thus in the East we see humanity doing everything possible to prepare a body or a corporality,—consisting of physical body, etheric body and astral body—into which could penetrate the Christ, He who, together with the ego-consciousness and by means of it, brings the impulse of Love to the earth. Love is that which, in its most psychic and spiritual form, came to the earth with Christ, appearing in its psychic and spiritual form in the East,—for thus we first see it—and then flowing on further, to the West, where it is understood. In this way do we see development progressing further.

In what way was the ego-consciousness able so to work in the West that it felt itself related to Christ ? What had happened to the souls who had prematurely taken up the ego-consciousness ?

The Egyptian-Chaldean people waited for the spiritual or Consciousness Soul before they developed the ego ; the Graeco-Latin peoples developed it in the Intellectual-Soul or soul of higher feeling; the culture of Northern Europe had prematurely developed the ego in the Sentient-Soul. That was in the human soul early in those countries; thus the Sentient-soul and the ego-consciousness worked together there in a different way than anywhere else in the world. In Northern Europe they first made themselves felt in the development of mankind. What was the result of the Ego-consciousness being firmly established in the Sentient-Soul in the European peoples, before a Christ had entered into the development of mankind, and before the latter had taken up what had been developed in Asia?

Because of this a force had been developed in the soul of man, together with the Sentient Soul, which could only have been developed through the Sentient-Soul being permeated with the ego-feeling while still quite virginal and uninfluenced by other civilisations. This permeation of the Sentient-Soul with the sense of self (the ego-sense) has grown into man's conscience. This accounts for the wonderful innocence of conscience! How does it speak? It speaks in the same way in the simplest and most primitive of men, as it does in the most complex soul. It says quite simply: that is right! that is wrong! without any theory or dogma. When it says: that is right, or that is wrong, what it tells us works with the might of an instinct or an urge. You will only find it developed in this way in the West. Therefore it throws its first rays like a rosy dawn, towards Greece and from thence towards Rome, where indeed we find it very strongly developed. We first meet with the word conscience,—conscientia—in the works of the Roman writers. Whereas among the Greeks we only find the first sporadic hints of it in Euripides, we find the Romans quite familiar with it, it had then become a word in general use. This is because of the influence of that strain of culture which came into being through the mutual inter-permeation of the Sentient-Soul and ego-feeling; for the ego-feeling, which lifts men up from the lowest to the highest, already speaks in the Sentient-Soul,—in which hitherto nothing spoke but instincts, desires and passions,—and speaks there like a voice from God, urging man to do what is right that he may press up to the higher ego.

In this way we can trace the first rise of conscience among the peoples of Europe. From thence it spreads its rays abroad to the other peoples of the Earth. Thus through a wise world-guidance, the humanity in one part of the world was so prepared that conscience could be added as a contribution to the whole collective development of humanity. We have now mentioned everything that can throw light upon conscience. We mentioned that indefinable attribute of conscience, its pressing forth from the depths of the soul. Conscience speaks like an urging impulse; but it is not an impulse. Those philosophers who so describe it, are far from hitting the mark. It speaks with the same power as does the Spiritual-Soul itself when it appears; but yet with elemental, original forces.

So, we see: Love appears on the earth in the East; Conscience in the West. The two belong together; as Christ appears in the East, so Conscience awakens in the West, that through it Christ may be accepted. In the simultaneous occurrence of the fact of the Christ-Event and the comprehension of it, and in the preparation for these two things in different parts of the Earth, we see the ruling of an infinite Wisdom guiding our development. We have thus indicated the past history of Conscience.

If we recollect what has often been emphasised,—that now, after the conclusion of Kali-Yuga, we are going through a transition in which new forces will have to be developed,—we shall easily understand that we are now faced with important questions regarding the further development of conscience. In the last lecture we strongly and clearly emphasised the fact that we are advancing towards a new Christ-Event, in that the soul will become capable of perceiving the Christ by means of a certain etheric clairvoyance, and of re-experiencing, in itself, the Event of Damascus. We are therefore justified in asking the question : What will happen as regards the parallel experience, that of the development of conscience, in the epochs towards which we are advancing ? We will go into this question next Sunday (8th May), for the best way of celebrating our White Lotus Day will be to point out the living nature of the movement of Spiritual Science, and to explain that the conscience of man is in a state of transition. We shall see that light can be thrown upon it from many different sides. The public lecture will treat the subject quite exoterically, but even in these lectures many a thing can now be mentioned, because they have been going on for a number of years. Conscience can be spoken of in a deep sense, as we have done to-day,—or quite exoterically as we shall do on Thursday,—or it may be gone into yet more profoundly. But it will be some time before we can do that.

LECTURE 7.

THE FURTHER DEVELOPMENT OF CONSCIENCE.[1]

Berlin, 8th May, 1910.

To-day, the 8th May, the Theosophical Society celebrates the Day of the White Lotus, which to the outer world is known, in the usual terminology of the day, as the death-day of the instigator of that Spiritual stream in which we now stand. To us it would seem more appropriate to select a different designation for to-day's festival, one taken from our knowledge of the Spiritual world and which should run more like this : 'The day of transition from an activity on the physical plane to one in the Spiritual worlds'. For to us it is not only an inner conviction in the ordinary sense of the words but an ever-increasing knowledge, that what the outer world calls death is but the passing from one form of work, from an activity stimulated by the impressions of the outer physical world, to one entirely stimulated by the Spiritual world. When to-day we remember the great instigator, H. P. Blavatsky, and the leading persons of her movement who have also now passed over into the Spiritual realm, let us in particular try to form a clear idea of what we ourselves must make of our Spiritual movement so that it may represent a continuation of that activity which she exercised on the physical plane as long as she remained on it ; so that on the one hand it may be a continuation of that activity and at the same time be possible for the Foundress herself to continue her work from the Spiritual world, both now and in the future. On such a day as this it is seemly that we should in a sense break away from our usual study of theosophical matters, and theosophical life, and should instead go through a sort of conscientious retrospect, a retrospect concerning what the tasks and duties the theosophical movement sets before us, and which may also lead us to a sort of prevision of what this movement should become in the future, and what we should do, and avoid doing.

What we are carrying on as the Theosophical movement came into the world as the result of certain quite special circumstances and certain historical necessities. You know that there was here no question, as in other Spiritual movements or unions of any sort,—of one or more persons determining to follow certain ideals according as the quality of their hearts and minds leads them to feel enthusiasm for these ideals, trying to enthuse other people and to induce them to form societies or unions for carrying these into practice. Not in this way should we view the Theosophical movement if we understand it aright. We only do this if we look upon it as an historical necessity of our present life :

[1] Dr. Steiner was forced later on to leave the Theosophical Society because of its Dogmatic Authority.

76

something which, regardless of what people feel or would like to feel about it, was bound to come, for it already lay in the womb of time, so to speak, and had to be brought to birth. In what way then may we regard the Theosophical movement ? It may be considered as a descent, a new descent of Spiritual life, of Spiritual wisdom and Spiritual forces, into the sensible physical world from the super-sensible ones. Such a descent had to take place for the further development of man, and must repeatedly take place in the future. It cannot of course be our task to-day to point out all the different great impulses through which Spiritual life has flowed down from the super-sensible worlds in order that the soul-life of man should be renewed when it had, so to speak, grown old ; but in the course of time this has frequently occurred. One thing, however, must be borne in mind.

In the primeval past, not long after the great Atlantean catastrophe which the traditions of the various countries record as the story of the Flood, came that impulse that we may describe as the inflow of Spiritual life that poured into the development of mankind through the Holy Rishis. Then came that other stream of Spiritual life that flowed down into man's evolution through Zarathustra or Zoroaster, and we find another stream of like nature in that which came to the old Israelites through the revelations of Moses. Finally, we have the greatest Impulse of all in that mighty inflow of Spiritual life poured into the physical world through the appearance on Earth of Christ-Jesus. This is by far the mightiest Impulse ever given in the past, and as we have repeatedly emphasised, it is greater than any that can at any future time come into the earth development. We have also repeatedly stated that new impulses must ever come ; new Spiritual life and a new way of understanding the old Spiritual life must flow into the development of mankind ; were it not for this, the tree of human development, which will grow green when humanity has attained the goal of its evolution, would wither and perish. The mighty Christ-Well of life out of which He poured into human development must, through the new Spiritual impulses flowing into our earth-life, be better and better understood.

As our own age, our nineteenth century drew near, the time came when human development once again required a new intervention, a new impulse. Once again new stimuli, new revelations, had to flow from the supersensible worlds into our physical world. This was a necessity, and ought to have been felt as such in the earth itself, and was so felt in those regions from which the life of earth is guided, the Spiritual regions ; only a short-sighted human observation could say : ' What is the use of these constantly fresh streams of perfectly new kinds of truths ? Why should there be constantly new knowledge and new life-impulses ? We have that which was given us in Christianity, for example, and with that we can go on quite simply in the old way ! ' From a higher standpoint this sort of observation is extremely egotistical. It really is ! The very fact that such egotistical remarks are so frequently made to-day by the very people who believe themselves to be good and religious, is all the stronger proof that a refreshing of our Spiritual life is wanted. How often we hear it said to-day : ' What is the use of new Spiritual movements ? We have our old traditions which have been preserved through the ages as far back as history records ; do not let us spoil those traditions by what these people say who always think they know best!' That is an egotistical expression of the human soul. Those who speak thus are not aware of this; they do not realise that they are only anxious about the demands of their own souls. In themselves they feel: 'We are quite satisfied with what we have!' And they establish the dogma, a dreadful dogma from the standpoint of conscience, 'If we are satisfied with our way, those who must learn from us, those who come after us, must learn to find satisfaction in the same way as we have. All must go on as we ourselves feel to be right, in accordance with our knowledge!' That way of talking is very, very frequently heard in the outer world. This does not merely come from the limitations of a narrow soul, but is connected with what we might call an egotistical bent of the human soul. In religious life souls may in reality be extremely egotistical, while wearing a mask of piety. Anyone who takes the question of the Spiritual development of mankind seriously, must, if he studies the world around him with understanding, become aware of one thing. He must see that the human soul is gradually breaking away more and more from the method in which for centuries men have contemplated the Christ-Impulse, that greatest Impulse in the development of mankind. I do not as a rule care to refer to contemporaneous matters, for what goes on in the external spiritual life to-day is for the most part too insignificant to appeal to the deeper side of a serious observer. For instance, it was impossible in Berlin, during the last few weeks, to pass a placarding column without seeing notices of a lecture entitled, 'Did Jesus live?' You probably all know that what led to this subject being discussed as it has been in the widest circles—sometimes with very radical weapons—was the view announced by a German Professor of Philosophy, Dr. Arthur Drews, a disciple of Edouard Hartmann, author of *The Philosophy of the Unknown* and more especially of *The Christ Myth*. The contents of the latter book have been made more widely known by the lecture given by Professor Drews here in Berlin, under the title: 'Did Jesus live?'

It is, of course, in no sense my task to enter into the particulars of that lecture. I will only put its principal thoughts before you. The author of *The Christ Myth*,—a modern philosopher who may be supposed to represent the science and thought of the day,—searches through the several records of olden times that are supposed to offer historical proof that a certain person of the name of Jesus of Nazareth lived at the beginning of our era. He then tries, by the help of what science and the critics have proved, to reduce the result of all this to something like the following question: 'Are the separate Gospels historic records proving that Jesus lived?' He takes all that Modern Theology on its part has to say, and then tries to show that none of the Gospels can be historic records and that it is impossible to prove by them that Jesus ever lived. He also tries to prove that none of the other records of a purely historical nature which man possesses are determinative, and that nothing conclusive concerning an historic Jesus can be deduced from them.

Now everyone who has gone into this question knows, that considered purely from an external standpoint, the sort of observation practised by Professor Drews has much in its favour, and comes as a sort of result of modern theological criticism. I will not go into details; for it is of no consequence to-day that someone having studied the philosophical side of science should assert that there is no historic document to prove that Jesus lived, because the only documents supposed to do so are not authoritative. Drews and all those of like mind go by what has come to us from Paul the Apostle. (In recent times there are even people who doubt the genuine character of all the Pauline Epistles, but as the author of *The Christ Myth* does not go so far as that, we need not go into it.) Drews says of St. Paul that he does not base his assertions on a personal acquaintance with Jesus of Nazareth, but on the revelation he received in the Event of Damascus. We know that this is absolutely true. But now Drews comes to the following conclusion : ' What concept of Christ did St. Paul hold ? He formed the concept of a purely Spiritual Christ, who can dwell in each human soul, so to speak, and can be realised within each one. St. Paul nowhere asserts the necessity that the Christ, whom he considered as a purely Spiritual Being, should have been present in a Jesus whose existence cannot be historically proved. One can therefore say : that no one knows whether an historic Jesus lived or not ; that the Christ-concept of St. Paul is a purely spiritual one, simply reproducing what may live in every human soul as an impulse towards perfection, as a sort of God in man.' The author of *The Christ Myth* further points out that certain conceptions—similar to the idea the Christians have of Jesus Christ—were already in existence concerning a sort of pre-Christian Jesus, and that several Eastern peoples had the concept of a Messiah. This compels Drews to ask : ' What then is actually the difference between the idea of Christ which St. Paul had [and which Drews does not attempt to deny],—what is the difference between the picture of Christ which St. Paul had in his heart and soul, and the idea of the Messiah already in existence ? ' Drews then goes on to say : ' Before the time of St. Paul, men had a Christ-picture of a God, a Messiah-picture of a God, who did not actually become man, who did not descend so far as individual manhood ; they even celebrated His suffering, death and resurrection as symbolical processes in their various festivals and mysteries ; but one thing they did not possess : there is no record of an individual man having really passed through suffering, death and resurrection on the physical earth.' That then was more or less the general idea—The author of *The Christ Myth* now asks : ' In how far then is there anything new in St. Paul ? To what extent did he carry the idea of Christ further ? '

Drews himself replies : ' The advance made by St. Paul on the earlier conceptions is that he does not represent a God hovering in the higher regions, but a God who became individual man.' Now I want you to note this : According to the author of *The Christ Myth*, Paul pictures a Christ who really became man. But the strange part is this : St. Paul is supposed to have stopped short at that idea ! He is supposed to have grasped the idea of a Christ Who really became man, although, according to him Christ never existed as such ! St. Paul is therefore supposed to say, that the highest idea possible is that of a God, a Christ, not only hovering in the higher regions, but having descended to earth and become man ; but it never entered his mind that this Christ actually did live on earth in a human being. This means that the author of *The Christ Myth* attributes to St. Paul a conception of the Christ which, to sound thinking

79

is a mockery. St. Paul is made to say : 'Christ must certainly have been an individual man, but although I preach Him, I deny His existence in any historical sense.'

That is the nucleus round which the whole subject turns ; truly one does not require much theological or critical erudition to refute it ; it is only necessary to confront Professor Drews as philosopher. For his Christ-concept cannot possibly stand. The Pauline Christ-concept, in the sense in which Drews takes it, cannot be maintained without accepting the historic Jesus. Professor Drews' book itself demands the existence of the historic Jesus. It would seem therefore, that at the present time a book can be accepted in the widest circles and considered as an earnest and scientific work, which is centred upon a contradiction such as turns all inner logic into a mockery ! Is it possible in these days for human thought to travel along such crooked paths as these ? What is the reason of this ? Anyone who wishes clearly to understand the development of mankind must find the answer to that question.

The reason is that what men believe or think at any given period, is not the result of their logical thought, but of their feelings and sentiments ; they believe and think what they wish to think. In particular do those who are preparing the Christ-concept for the coming age feel a strong impulse to shut out from their hearts everything to be found in the old external records—and yet they also feel an urge to prove everything by means of such external documents. These however, considered from a purely material standpoint, lose their value after a definite lapse of time. The time will come for Shakespeare, just as it came for Homer, so will it come for Goethe, when people will try to prove that an historic Goethe never existed at all. Historic records must in course of time lose their value from a material standpoint. What then is necessary, seeing that we are already living in an age when the thought of its most prominent representatives is such that they have an impulse in their hearts urging them towards the denial of the historic Christ ? What is necessary as a new impulse of Spiritual life ? It is necessary that the possibility should be given of understanding the historic Jesus in a spiritual way. In what other way can this fact be expressed ?

As we all know, St. Paul started from the Event of Damascus. We also know that to him that Event was the great revelation, whereas all he had heard at Jerusalem—on the physical plane, as direct information—had not been able to make a Saul into St. Paul. What convinced him was the Damascus revelation from Spiritual worlds ! Through that alone Christianity really came into being, and through that St. Paul gained the power to proclaim the Christ. But did he obtain a purely abstract idea, which in itself might be contradicted ? No ! He was convinced from what he had seen in the Spiritual worlds that Christ had lived on earth, had suffered, died and risen. 'If Christ be not risen then is my teaching vain,' St. Paul quite rightly said. He did not receive the mere idea, the concept of Christ from the Spiritual worlds, he convinced himself of the reality of the Christ, Who died on Golgotha. To him that was proof of the historic Jesus.

What then is necessary, now that the time is approaching when, as a result of the materialism of the age the historic records are losing their value, when

80

everyone can quite easily prove that these records cannot withstand criticism, so that nothing can be proved externally and historically ? It is necessary that people should learn that Christ can be recognised as the historic Jesus without any external records whatever, that through a right training the Event of Damascus can be renewed in each human being and indeed in the near future will be renewed for humanity as a whole, so that it is absolutely possible to be convinced of the existence of an historic Jesus. That is the new way in which the world must find the road to Him. It is of no consequence whether the facts that occurred were right or wrong, the point of importance is that they did occur. It is of no consequence that such a book as *The Christ Myth* should contain certain errors, the thing that matters is, it was found possible to write it ! It shows that quite different methods are necessary in order that Christ may remain with humanity ; that He may be rediscovered.

A man who thinks about humanity and its needs and of how the souls of men are expressing themselves externally, will not adopt the standpoint of saying : ' What do those people who think differently matter to me ? I have my own convictions, they are quite enough for me.' Most people do not realise what dreadful egoism underlies such words. It was not as the result of an idea, an outer ideal, or of any personal predilection, that a movement arose through which people might learn that it is possible to find the way into the spiritual world, and that among other things, Christ Himself can also be found there. This movement came into being in response to a necessity which arose in the course of the nineteenth century, that there should flow down from the spiritual worlds into the physical world, possibilities, by means of which men will be able to obtain spiritual truth in a new sort of way, the old way having died out. In the course of the past winter, have we not testified how fruitful this new way may be ?

We have repeatedly laid stress on the fact that the first thing for us in our movement is not to take our stand on any record or external document, but first of all to enquire : What is revealed to clairvoyant consciousness when one ascends to the spiritual worlds ? If, through some catastrophe, all the historical proofs of the historic Jesus of the Gospels and of the Epistles of St. Paul were lost, what would independent spiritual consciousness tell us ? What do we learn concerning the spiritual worlds on the path which can be trodden any day and hour by each one ? We are told : ' In the Spiritual worlds you will find the Christ, even though you know nothing historically of the fact that He was on the earth at the beginning of our era.'

The fact which must be established over and over again by a renewal of the Event of Damascus is that there is an original proof of the historic personality of Jesus of Nazareth ! Just as a school-boy is not told that he must believe the three sides of a triangle make a hundred and eighty degrees simply because in olden times that was laid down as a fact, but is made to prove it for himself,—so we to-day, not only testify out of a spiritual consciousness that Christ has always existed, but also that the historic Jesus can be found in the spiritual worlds, that He is a reality, and was a reality at the very time of which tradition tells.

We have gone further and have shown that what we established by spiritual perception without the Gospels, is to be rediscovered within them. We then feel a deep respect and reverence for the Gospels for we find again in them what we found in the spiritual worlds independently of them. We now know that they must have come from the same sources of supersensible illumination from which we must draw to-day ; we know they must be records of the spiritual worlds.

The purpose of what we call the Theosophical movement is to make such a method of observation possible, to make it possible for spiritual life to play its part in human science. In order that this might come about, the stimulus thereto had to be given by the Theosophical Society. That is the one side of the question. The other is that this stimulus had to be given at a time which was least ripe for it. This is proved by the fact that to-day, thirty years after the birth of the Theosophical movement, the story of the non-historic Jesus still endures. How much is known, outside this movement, of the possibility of the historic Jesus being discovered in any other way than through the external documents ? What was being done in the nineteenth century still continues : the authority of the religious documents is being undermined. Thus while there was the greatest necessity that this new possibility should be given to humanity—on the other hand the preparations made for its reception were the smallest conceivable. For do we by any chance believe that our modern philosophers are particularly ready to receive it ? How little ready the philosophers of the twentieth century are, can be seen by the concept they have of the Christ of St. Paul. Anyone acquainted with scientific life knows that this is the great and final result of the materialism which has been preparing for centuries : although it asserts that it wishes to rise above materialism, the mode of thought prevailing in science has not progressed beyond that which is in process of dying out. Science as it exists to-day certainly is a ripe fruit, but one which must suffer the fate of all ripe fruit ; it must begin to decay. No one can assert that it could bring forth a new impulse for the renewal of its mode of thought or of its methods of coming to conclusions. When we think of this we realise, apart from all other considerations, the weight of the stimulus given through H. P. Blavatsky ;—no matter what our opinions of her capacities and the details of her life may be, she was the instrument for the giving of the stimulus ; and she proved herself fully competent for the purpose.— We who are taking part in celebrating such a day as this, as members of the Theosophical Society, are in a very peculiar position. We are celebrating a personal festival, dedicated to one person. Now, although the belief in Authority is certainly a dangerous thing in the external world, yet there the danger is reduced by reason of the jealousy and envy that play so great a part ; even though the reverence of a few persons is manifested outwardly, and rather strongly, by the burning of incense, yet egoism and envy has considerable power over them. In the Theosophical movement the danger of injury through the worship of the personality and belief in Authority is particularly great. We are, therefore, in a very peculiar position when we celebrate a festival dedicated to a personality. Not only the customs of the time but also the matter itself places us in a difficult position, for the revelations of the higher worlds must always come along the by-way of the personality. Personalities must be the bearers of the revelations—and yet we must take care not to confuse the former with the latter. We must receive the revelations through the medium of a personality, and the question that constantly recurs whether he or she is worthy of confidence, is a very natural one :' What they did on such and such a day does not harmonise with our ideas ! Can we, therefore, believe in the whole thing ? '

This forms part of a certain tendency of our time, which we may describe as lack of devotion to the truth. How often at the present day do we hear of a case in which some prominent person may please the public ; for one or more decades what he or she does may be quite satisfactory, for the public is too lazy to go into the matter for itself. Some years after, if it should transpire that this person's private life is not all it might be and open to suspicion, the idol then falls to the ground. Whether this is right or not is not the point. The point is that we ought to acquire a feeling that although the person in question may be the means by which the spiritual life comes to us, it is our duty to prove this for ourselves—and indeed to test the person by the truth, instead of testing the truth by the person. Especially should that be our attitude in the Theosophical movement ; we pay most respect to a personality if we do not encumber him with belief in Authority, as people are so fond of doing, for we know that the activity of that personality after death is only transferred to the spiritual world. We are justified in saying that the activity of H. P. Blavatsky still continues, and we, within the movement which she instigated, can either further that activity or injure it. Most of all do we injure it if we blindly believe in her, swearing by what she thought when she lived on the physical plane, and blindly believing in her authority. We revere and help her most if we are fully conscious that she provided the stimulus for a movement which originated from one of the deepest necessities in human evolution. While we see that this movement had to come, we ascribe the stimulus to her ; but many years have gone by since that time and we must prove ourselves worthy of her work, by acknowledging that what was then started must now be carried further. We admit that it had to be instigated by her, but do not let us ferret about in her private affairs, especially at the present time. We know the significance of the impetus she gave, but we know that it only very imperfectly represents what is to come. When we recollect all that has been put before our souls during the past winter, we cannot but say : What Madame Blavatsky started is indeed of deep and incisive importance, but how immeasurable is all that she could not accomplish in that introductory act of hers ! What has just been said of the necessity of the Theosophical Movement for the Christ-experience was completely hidden from Blavatsky. Her task was to point out the germs of truth in the religions of the Aryan peoples ; the comprehension of the revelations given in the Old and New Testaments was denied her. We honour the positive work accomplished by this Personality and we shall not refer to all she was not able to do, all that was concealed from her and which we must now contribute. Anyone who allows himself to be stirred by H. P. Blavatsky and wishes to go further than she, will say : If the stimulus given by her in the Theosophical Movement is to be carried further, we must attain to an understanding of the Christ-Event.

The early Theosophical movement failed to grasp the religious and spiritual life of the Old and New Testaments; that is why everything is wide of the mark in this first movement, and the Theosophical Movement has the task of making this good and of adding what was not given at first. If we inwardly feel these facts, they are as it were a claim, made by our Theosophical conscience.

Thus we visualise H. P. Blavatsky as the bringer of a sort of dawn of a new light; but of what good would that light be if it were not to illuminate the most important thing that mankind has ever possessed! A Theosophy which does not provide the means of understanding Christianity is absolutely value-less to our present civilisation; but if it should become an instrument for the understanding of Christianity we should then be making the right use of the instrument. If we do not do this, if we do not use the impulse given by H. P. Blavatsky for this purpose, what are we doing? We are arresting the activity of her spirit in our age! Everything is in course of development, including the spirit of Blavatsky. Her spirit is now working in the spiritual world to further the progress of the Theosophical movement; but if we sit before her and the book she wrote, saying: 'We will raise a monument to you consisting of your own works,'—who is it that is making her spirit earth-bound? Who is con-demning her not to progress beyond what she established on earth? We, our-selves! We revere and acknowledge her value if, even as she herself went beyond her time, we also go further than she did so long as the grace ruling the development of the world continues to vouchsafe spiritual revelations from the spiritual world.

That is what we place before our souls to-day as a question of conscience, and after all that is most in accordance with the wishes of our comrade H. C. Olcott, the first President of the Theosophical Society, who has also now passed into the spiritual world. Let us inscribe this in our souls to-day, for it is pre-cisely through lack of knowledge of the living Theosophical life that all the shadow-sides of the Theosophical movement have arisen. If the Theosophical movement were to carry out its great original impulse, unweakened, and with a holy conscience, it would possess the force to drive out of the field all the harm-ful influences which, as time went by, have already come in, as well as others which certainly will come. This one thing we must very earnestly do: we must continue to develope the impulse. In many places to-day we see Theoso-phists who think they are doing good work, and who feel very happy to be able to say: 'We are now doing something which is in conformity with external science!' How pleasing it is to many leading Theosophists if they can point out that those who study various religions confirm what has come from the spiritual world; while they quite fail to observe that it is just this unspiritual mode of comparison that must be overcome. For instance Theosophy comes into close contact with the thoughts which led to the denial of the historic Jesus and indeed there is a certain relation between them. Originally Theoso-phy only ranked the historic Jesus with other founders of religion. It never occurred to Blavatsky to deny the historic Jesus; though she certainly placed Him one hundred years earlier. She did not deny His existence, but she did not recognise Christ-Jesus; although she instigated the movement in which He may some day be known, she was not able herself to recognise Him. In this, the first state of the Theosophical movement comes strangely into line with what those who deny the historic Jesus are doing to-day.

For instance, Professor Drews points out that the occurrences that preceded the Event of Golgotha can also be found in the accounts of the old Gods, for example in the cult of Adonis or Tammuz, in that there is a suffering God-hero, a dying God-hero and a risen God-hero, and so on. What is contained in the various religious traditions is always being brought forward and the following conclusion drawn : you are told of a Jesus of Nazareth, who suffered, died and rose again and who was the Christ ; but you see that other peoples also worshipped an Adonis, a Tammuz, etc. The similarity to one of the old gods is constantly being insisted on, when referring to the occurrences in Palestine.

This is also being done in our Theosophical movement. People do not realise that comparing the religions of Adonis or Tammuz with the events in Palestine proves nothing. I will show you by means of an example wherein such comparisons are at fault ; on the surface they may work out all right, yet there is a great flaw in them. Suppose an official living in 1910 wore a certain uniform as an outer sign of his official activity ; and that in 1930 a totally different man should wear the same uniform. It will not be the uniform but the individual wearing it that determines the efficiency of the work he accomplishes. Now, suppose that in the year 2090 an historian comes forward and says : ' I have ascertained that in 1910 there lived a man who wore a particular coat, waistocat and trousers and further, that in 1930 the same uniform was being worn, we see therefore, that the coat, waistcoat and trousers have been carried over and that on both occasions we have the same being before us.'

Such a conclusion would of course be foolish, but not more so than to say that in the religions of Asia Minor we find Adonis or Tammuz undergoing suffering and death and rising again, and that we find the same in Christ ! The point is not that suffering, death and resurrection were experienced, the point is by Whom were they experienced ! Suffering, death and resurrection are like a uniform in the historical development of the world and we should not point to the uniform we meet with in the legends, but to the individualities who wore it. It is true that individualities, in order that men might understand them, have so to say performed Christ-deeds which show that they too could accomplish the acts of a Tammuz, for instance ; but each time there was a different being behind the acts. Therefore, all comparisons of religions proving that the figure of Siegfried corresponds to that of Baldur, Baldur to Tammuz and so on, are but a sign that the legends and myths take certain forms in certain peoples. When we are trying to gain knowledge of man there is no more value in these comparisons than there would be in pointing out that a certain species of uniform is later found to be in use for the same office. That is the fundamental error prevailing everywhere, even in the Theosophical movement, and it is nothing but a result of the materialistic habit of thought.

The will and testament of Blavatsky will only be fulfilled if the Theosophical movement is able to cultivate and preserve the life of the spirit—if it looks to the spirit which shows itself, and not in the books someone may have written. Spirit should be cultivated among us. We will not merely study books written centuries ago, but develop in a living way the spirit which has been given us. We will be a union of persons who do not simply believe in books or in individuals, but in the living spirit; who do not merely talk about H. P. Blavatsky having departed from the physical plane and continuing to live on after her death, but who believe in such a living way in what has been revealed through Theosophy that her life on the physical plane may not be made a hindrance to the further supersensible activity of her spirit.

Only when we think about her in that way will the Theosophical movement be of use, and only when men and women who think in that way are to be found on the earth can H. P. Blavatsky do anything for the movement. For this it is necessary that further spiritual research should be made, and above all that people should learn what was asserted in the last public lecture :— that mankind is in process of development and that something approximate to conscience came into being at the time of Jesus Christ; that such things do arise and are of significance to the whole of evolution. At a particular point of time conscience arose; before that time it was altogether a different thing, and it will be different again after man's soul has for some while developed further in the light of conscience. We have already indicated the way in which it will alter in the future.

As a parallel to the appearance of the Event of Damascus a great number of people in the course of the twentieth century will experience something like the following : As soon as they have acted in some way they will learn to contemplate their deed; they will become more thoughtful, they will have an inner picture of the deed. At first only a few people will experience this, but the numbers will continually increase during the next two or three thousand years. As soon as they have done something the picture will be there; at first they will not know what it is; but those who have studied Theosophy will say : ' This is a picture ! It is no dream; it is a picture, showing the karmic fulfilment of the act I have just committed. Some day this will take place as the fulfilment, the karmic balancing of what I have just done ! ' This will begin in the twentieth century. Man will begin to develop the faculty of seeing before him a picture of a far-distant, not-yet-accomplished act. It will show itself as an inner counterpart of his action, its karmic fulfilment, which will some day take place. Man will then be able to say : ' I have now been shown what I shall have to do to compensate for what I have just done, and I can never become perfect until I have made that compensation.' Karma will then cease to be mere theory, for this inner picture will be experienced.

Such faculties as this are becoming more frequent; new capacities are developing; but the old are the germs for the new. What will make it possible for men to be shown the karmic pictures ? It will come as a result of the soul having for some time stood in the light of conscience ! Not the various external physical experiences it may have are of most importance to the soul, but rather its progress towards perfection. By the help of conscience the soul is now preparing for what has been just described. The more incarnations a man has during which he cultivates and perfects his conscience, the more he is doing towards acquiring that higher faculty through which in the form of spiritual vision the voice of God will once more speak to him, the voice of God which was formerly experienced in a different way. Æschylos still represented his Orestes as having a vision before him of what had been brought about by his evil actions; he was compelled to see the results of these actions in the external world. The new capacity in course of development for the soul is such that men will see the effects of their deeds in pictures of the future. That is the new stage. Development runs its course in cycles, following a circular movement, and what man possessed in his older vision comes back again in a new form.

Through knowledge of the spiritual world we are really preparing to awake in the right way in our next incarnation, and this knowledge also helps us to work in the right way for those who are to come after us. For this reason Theosophy is in itself no egotistical movement, for it does not concern itself with what benefits the individual alone but with what makes for the progress of all mankind.

We have now enquired on two occasions: 'What is conscience?' To-day we have also asked: 'What will the conscience now developing, eventually become? How does conscience stand, if we regard it as a seed in the age through which we are now passing? What will be the result of the action of this seed of conscience?—The higher faculties just described!' It is very important that we should believe in the evolution of the soul, from incarnation to incarnation, from age to age. We learn that, when we learn to understand true Christianity. In this respect we still have a great deal to learn from St. Paul. In all Eastern religions, even in Buddhism, you find the doctrine that 'the outer world is Maya.' So it is; and in the East that is established as absolute truth. St. Paul points to the same truth, and emphatically asserts it. At the same time St. Paul emphasises something else: 'Man does not see the truth when he looks with his eyes; he does not see the reality when he looks at what is outside. Why is this? Because, in his descent into matter he himself transfused the external reality with illusion. It is man himself, through his own act, who made the outer world an illusion.' Whether you call this the Fall, as the Bible does, or give it any other name, it is a man's own fault that the outer world now appears as an illusion. Eastern religions attribute the blame for this to the Gods! 'Beat thy breast,' says St. Paul, 'for thou hast descended and so dimmed thy vision that colour and sound no longer appear spiritual. Dost thou believe that colour and sound are materially existent? They are Maya! Thou thyself hast made them Maya. Thou, man, must release thyself from this; thou must re-acquire what thou hast done away with! Thou hast descended into matter and now must thou release thyself therefrom, and set thyself free—though not in the way advised by Buddha: Free thyself from the longing for existence! No! Thou must look upon the life on earth in its true light. What thou thyself hast reduced to Maya, that thou must restore within thee—This thou can'st do by taking into thyself the Christ-force, which will show thee the outer world in its reality!'

Herein lies a great impulse for the life of the countries of the West, a new impulse, which as yet is far from having been carried into all parts. What does the world know to-day of the fact that in one part of it an endeavour is actually being made to create a 'theory of Knowledge' in the sense of St. Paul, as it were ? Such a theory could not affirm as Kant does : 'The thing-in-itself is incomprehensible.' Such a theory of knowledge could only say : 'It lies with thee, O man ; through what thou now art, thou art bringing about an untrue reality. Thou must thyself go through an inner process. Then will Maya be transformed into truth, into spiritual reality !' The task of both my books, *Truth and Science* and *The Philosophy of Spiritual Activity*, was to put the theory of Knowledge on a Pauline basis. Both these books are focussed on that which is the great achievement of the Pauline conception of man in the Western world. The reason these books are so little understood, or at most in theosophical circles, is because they assume the hypothesis of the whole impulse which has found expression in the Theosophical movement. The greatest must be seen in the smallest !

Through such considerations as these, which lift us above the limits of our narrow humanity, and show us how, in our little every-day work, we can link on to that which goes on from stage to stage, from life to life, leading us ever more and more into the spiritual existence,—through dwelling on these we shall become good Theosophists. It is right that we should devote ourselves to thoughts such as these, on a day devoted to a personality who gave the stimulus to a movement that will live on and on, which is not to remain a mere colourless theory but must have the sap of life within it, so that the tree of the theosophical conception of the world may constantly renew its greenness.

In this spirit let us endeavour to make ourselves capable of preparing a field in the Theosophical movement in which the impulse of Blavatsky shall not be hindered and arrested, but shall progress to further development.